SAVING GRACE

A GUIDE TO FINANCIAL WELL-BEING

CLERGY WORKBOOK

Clergy Sections by Alex Joyner

Abingdon Press™

Nashville

Saving Grace
A Guide to Financial Well-Being
Clergy Workbook

978-1-7910-0837-6

20 21 22 23 24 25 26 27 28 29—10 9 8 7 6 5 4 3 2 1
MANUFACTURED IN THE UNITED STATES OF AMERICA

Contents

Introduction

There's no question that money is a big day-to-day issue in all our lives—regardless of how much of it we have. In fact, if you add up the hours we spend making it, spending it, worrying about it, fighting over it, trying to protect it, and trying to manage it, you would find that we spend a lot of our waking hours focused on money. It's a big issue, one that affects most aspects of our lives.

Wealth is a constant theme in the Old Testament, Jesus spoke about money multiple times in his teachings, and some of John Wesley's most memorable sermons include the importance of how we earn, save, and give our money. Money is a powerful thing. Some even say that money is more than just a neutral medium that can be used for good or for bad; they would argue that money has a spiritual force or power and that power is reinforced by myths that have become a powerful force in shaping the materialistic, consumer-focused culture in which we find ourselves.

We are all affected by the myths of our consumer culture as they relate to money; and in this study we will examine many of these myths and contrast them with a more faithful way to understand money and how we spend and interact with it. In order to follow this faithful way toward financial well-being, we get very practical about it, using tools and biblical principles and applying them to our everyday lives with money. This study presents a grace-filled and faith-based way to approach your finances and helps you counter the myths of today's American consumer culture.

In addition to Scripture and practical financial advice, we also have Christian leaders and theologians from the past to guide us with important insights about how to earn, save, and give our money in a way that is faithful to God. One such theologian is John Wesley, a priest in the Church of England in the eighteenth century who founded the Methodist movement. His teachings, practices, and theology are a part of the heritage of many Christian denominations today, including The United Methodist Church. Wesley firmly believed and taught that the Christian faith must be lived, that our faithfulness to God is ultimately expressed in the habits, practices, behaviors, and attitudes that characterize our lives. Money was no exception, and in a number of his works Wesley described a faithful relationship with money in which it is a tool that can be used to express our love of God and neighbor. Throughout this workbook, you will find examples and quotations from John Wesley to enhance and illuminate teaching from the Bible about what it means to experience financial freedom.

Whether you are just starting out or already have a budgeting system in place, the goal of this study is for you to become grounded in a biblical understanding of a sound relationship to money and to develop and commit to a biblically based Spending Plan for your household. We want to help you manage your money, as opposed to it managing you, so that you experience a sense of grace, peace, and contentment about your finances. In that spirit, we will be exploring money management from the standpoint that wise choices can bring you to a place of well-being and order in an area of our lives where that is often not the case.

We hope this study will be more than just a learning experience about spending plans, finances, and your relationship to money. We hope it will also be a time for you to reflect on your relationship to God, because our relationship to money is closely related to our relationship to God.

Second, we hope to offer practical tools and skills that will enable you to manage and control your finances. We want you to gain the skills to master your money so you can experience grace and well-being in this area of your life, perhaps like you have never known before. We want you to finish this study with a Spending Plan in your hand, the knowledge in your head to implement it, and the desire and motivation in your heart to follow through on it.

How This Study Works

Study Overview

In this study, we will:

- Contrast what the consumer culture says about money with what the Bible says about money.
- Show you how to track your expenses and evaluate your income.
- Discuss giving and saving.
- Address your debt.
- Walk you through creating a personal Spending Plan that will guide every aspect of your financial life.
- Encourage you in ways to experience grace, peace, and joy in your financial life.

You can do this study alone, with a partner, or as a part of a small group. In each session, we'll explore a different aspect of our financial lives. We'll identify the pull of our consumer culture in each area and explore how the faithful way can guide our decisions. Throughout the sessions, there are activities in which you can interact and jot down your thoughts and actions to take in each area, and each session will walk you through completing a section of your Spending Plan.

Note that this study contains a substantial appendix on pages 129–168 and CAP-1–CAP-3 of this workbook. These materials include additional tips for completing and following your Spending Plan, along with further financial information and resources.

First, A Little Homework

This study contains a number of pre-work forms that are designed to gather information and set you up for success in a new approach to your financial life. In order for the study to be as valuable and productive as possible, it is very important that you complete the pre-work forms prior to beginning the study. This is the only time you will need to complete these forms and the only time you will need to dedicate a significant amount of time to working before class sessions. Don't be intimidated! Completing the forms may take some time, but the work will set the stage for a rich and meaningful study toward your financial well-being. It's good to get started as soon as possible. If you are participating in a small group, the information you are asked to collect is confidential, and no one else will see it. Throughout the study, you will use your pre-work information to inform your personal Spending Plan.

Pre-Work Instructions

Six worksheets are included in the pre-work to help you prepare for the study. If you are completing this study as part of a small group, please allow plenty of time prior to the study to gather the information and to complete each form. Additional copies of the worksheets (as well as many of the forms used in this workbook) can be found in PDF format at abingdonpress.com/savinggrace or at AmplifyMedia.com by searching "Saving Grace." For those who prefer an interactive form of the worksheets, the website also has PDF versions available that will perform the calculations in the exercises for you. Instructions to help you complete each form are listed below.

Goals to Achieve this Year

Make it a priority to reflect on your financial goals. If you are sharing finances with a partner, discuss your financial goals together. These goals will become the basis for shaping your Spending Plan, and they will provide motivation for following through on your decisions in the months ahead.

What I Owe / What I Own

As you fill out the second column (Amount) of this form, enter the amount of the total balance due on each item.

The "What I Own" section is optional, but we encourage you to fill it out so you can calculate a simplified version of your net worth. Consider the value of things you own to be the amount you would expect to get if you sold the items.

Gift List

Gifts are an often overlooked or underestimated part of spending. Write the names of individuals you will be purchasing gifts for in the coming year. Remember to include cards, postage at Christmas, and parties. You may wish to include some money for as-yet-unannounced weddings, showers, or other special events.

What I Spend

This worksheet will evolve into your master Spending Plan, but for now, use it to enter what you are currently spending.

Gather as much information as you can to determine a monthly average for what you spend in each category. Going through your written records, online bank account, and your credit card statements for the past year will be helpful. Even if you have not kept written records, you can reconstruct your expense history using online sources. Be sure to include periodic expense items such as auto insurance or taxes that may not be paid on a monthly basis. If you have not kept records in the past, some of the categories may be difficult to estimate. Give it your best shot, recognizing that if you don't have records showing how much you're spending in a particular area, the amount is probably more than you think it is.

The income figures at the top of the page should be your monthly take-home pay after taxes and other deductions. Make a note of any deductions (such as medical insurance or retirement contributions). Where those items occur under expenses, enter the notation "payroll deduction."

If your income varies from month to month, use a conservative monthly estimate based on the last two or three years' earnings. Referring back to your income tax records could be helpful in making this determination. Remember, you are looking for after-tax, take-home income. This is called your "net income."

Money Motivation Quiz

This exercise will provide insightful information on your behavior regarding money. If you are working through this study as a couple, be sure to have each partner take the quiz. Keep the results in mind as you analyze your financial choices in this study.

Money Autobiography

The Money Autobiography can also provide insight into why we handle money as we do. All of us have been influenced by how money was handled in our homes growing up—sometimes for better, sometimes for worse. Reflecting on the questions asked in the Money Autobiography can raise our consciousness of those influences and help us take steps to counteract any that may have been negative

Clergy Sections

This Clergy Workbook contains three sections with specific information and reflection on the unique aspects of clergy finances. In these sections, you can find helpful information to guide you in thinking through taxes, housing allowances, retirement benefits, and other considerations as a clergyperson, as well as your role and responsibility in being a financial leader for your congregation. You can find the first section at the end of chapter 2; the second section at the end of chapter 4; and the third section at the end of chapter 6. As you go through the workbook, read these sections carefully as you come to them, and reflect on the discussion questions at the end. At the back of the book, there is a Clergy Appendix that lists specific benefits and resources for United Methodist clergy.

It is recommended that you work through this program in a discussion group with other clergy members. Leave some extra time during your second, fourth, and sixth sessions to talk together about these clergy sections and their implications for your finances. There are three short videos to introduce this material and begin your discussion. You can find these videos, featuring Phil and Janet Jamieson, at AmplifyMedia.com (search Saving Grace), or on the *Saving Grace* DVD.

NEED EXTRA WORKSHEETS OR FORMS

Additional copies of the worksheets and forms in this workbook can be found in PDF format at abingdonpress .com/savinggrace or AmplifyMedia. com by searching "Saving Grace." For those who may prefer an interactive form of the worksheets, the website also offers PDF versions that will perform the calculations in the exercises for you.

WORKSHEET #1: GOALS TO ACHIEVE THIS YEAR

Please allow adequate time to give serious consideration to your goals. Carefully considered, realistic goals that flow out of what's really important to you are powerful motivators. That motivation will be very helpful to you in following through on the steps necessary to achieve your goals and ultimately, financial freedom!

Overall Goal

State your overall goal in starting this course. What do you hope will happen as a result?

My Goal:

Specific Goals to Achieve

Following are some possible goals that can serve as "thought starters" for you. The important thing is that the goals you list are ones that are truly important to you. Be as specific as you can, using dates, amounts, etc.

Pay off debt: _____

Save for: _____
(major purchase, replacement items, college, retirement)

Increase my giving to: _____

Become more disciplined in: _____

Other: _____

Other: _____

Other: _____

WORKSHEET #2: WHAT I OWE / WHAT I OWN

What I Owe				What I Own (optional)	
I Owe (Liabilities)	Amount	Minimum Monthly Payments	Interest Percentage*	I Own (Assets)	Amount
Mortgage (current balance)				Checking Account	
Home Equity Loans				Savings Account	
Credit Cards				Other Savings	
				Insurance (cash value)	
				Retirement	
				Home (market value)	
Car Loans				Auto (market value)	
Education Loans				Second Auto (market value)	
Family/Friends					
Other				Money Owed to Me	
				Other	
				Other	
Total of All I Owe				Total of All I Own	

*Note: Enter percents as .03 for 3%, .10 for 10%, etc.

Net Worth (optional)

Total of All I Own – Total of All I Owe = Net Worth (in earthly terms, not God's!)*

$ _____ – $ _____ = $ _____

*Never confuse your self-worth with your net worth. In God's eyes each one of us is of infinite worth.

WORKSHEET #3: GIFT LIST

List the names of those for whom you buy gifts and the amounts you typically spend on each occasion.*

Name	Birthday	Christmas	Anniversary	Other
1.				
2.				
3.				
4.				
5.				
6.				
7.				
8.				
9.				
10.				
11.				
12.				
13.				
14.				
15.				
16.				
17.				
18.				
19.				
20.				
Total				

Grand Total (of all columns) $ _____

Monthly Average (Total ÷ 12) = $ _____

*You may wish to also include the cost of holiday decorations, entertaining, etc.

WORKSHEET #4: WHAT I SPEND

What I Spend

Earnings/Income Per Month	Totals
Salary #1 (net take-home)	_____
Salary #2 (net take-home)	_____
Other (less taxes)	_____
Total Monthly Income	$ _____

% Guide*

1. Giving		$ _____
Church	_____	
Other Contributions	_____	

2. Savings	15%	$ _____
Emergency	_____	
Replacement	_____	
Long Term	_____	

3. Debt	0-10%	$ _____
Credit Cards:		
Visa	_____	
MasterCard	_____	
Discover	_____	
American Express	_____	
Gas Cards	_____	
Department Stores	_____	
Education Loans	_____	
Other Loans:		
Bank Loans	_____	
Credit Union	_____	
Family/Friends	_____	
Other	_____	

4. Housing	25-36%	$ _____
Mortgage/Taxes/Rent	_____	
Maintenance/Repairs	_____	
Utilities:		
Electric	_____	
Gas	_____	
Water	_____	
Trash and Recycling	_____	
Telephone/Internet	_____	
TV/Streaming Services	_____	
Other	_____	

5. Auto/Transp.	15-20%	$ _____
Car Payments/License	_____	
Gas & Bus/Train/Parking	_____	
Oil/Lube/Maintenance	_____	

* This is a percent of total monthly income. These are guidelines only and may be different for individual situations. However, there should be good rationale for a significant variance.

6. Insurance (Paid by you)	5%	$ _____
Auto	_____	
Homeowners	_____	
Life	_____	
Medical/Dental	_____	
Other	_____	

7. Household/Personal	15-25%	$ _____
Groceries	_____	
Clothes/Dry Cleaning	_____	
Gifts	_____	
Household Items	_____	
Personal:		
Tobacco & Alcohol	_____	
Cosmetics	_____	
Barber/Beauty	_____	
Other:		
Books/Magazines/Music	_____	
Allowances	_____	
Personal Technology	_____	
Extracurricular Activities	_____	
Education	_____	
Pets	_____	
Miscellaneous	_____	

8. Entertainment	5-10%	$ _____
Going Out:		
Meals	_____	
Movies/Events	_____	
Babysitting	_____	
Travel (Vacation/Trips)	_____	
Other:		
Fitness/Sports	_____	
Hobbies	_____	
Media Subscriptions	_____	
Other	_____	

9. Prof. Services	5-15%	$ _____
Child Care	_____	
Medical/Dental/Prescriptions	_____	
Other:		
Legal	_____	
Counseling	_____	
Professional Dues	_____	

10. Misc. Small Cash Expenditures	2-3%	$ _____

Total Expenses $ _____

TOTAL MONTHLY INCOME	$ _____
LESS TOTAL EXPENSES	$ _____
INCOME OVER/(UNDER) EXPENSES	$ _____

WORKSHEET #5: MONEY MOTIVATION QUIZ

Directions

For each of the questions below, circle the letter that best describes your response. There are no right or wrong answers here, just more insight into why you see and interact with money the way that you do.

1. Money is important because it allows me to . . .
   a. Do what I want to do.
   b. Feel secure.
   c. Get ahead in life.
   d. Buy things for others.

2. I feel that money . . .
   a. Frees up my time.
   b. Can solve my problems.
   c. Is a means to an end.
   d. Helps make relationships smoother.

3. When it comes to saving money, I . . .
   a. Don't have a plan and rarely save.
   b. Have a plan and stick to it.
   c. Don't have a plan but manage to save anyway.
   d. Don't make enough money to save.

4. If someone asks about my personal finances, I . . .
   a. Feel defensive.
   b. Realize I need more education and information.
   c. Feel comfortable and competent.
   d. Would rather talk about something else.

5. When I make a major purchase, I . . .
   a. Go with what my intuition tells me.
   b. Research a great deal before buying.
   c. Feel I'm in charge—it's my/our money.
   d. Ask friends/family first.

6. If I have money left over at the end of the month, I . . .
   a. Go out and have a good time.
   b. Put the money into savings.
   c. Look for a good investment.
   d. Buy a gift for someone.

7. If I discover I paid more for something than a friend did, I . . .
   a. Couldn't care less.
   b. Feel it's OK because I also find bargains at times.
   c. Assume they spent more time shopping, and time is money.
   d. Feel upset and angry with myself.

8. When paying bills, I . . .
   a. Put it off and sometimes forget.
   b. Pay them when due, but no sooner.
   c. Pay when I get to it, but don't want to be hassled.
   d. Worry that my credit will suffer if I miss a payment.

9. When it comes to borrowing money, I . . .
   a. Simply won't/don't like to feel indebted.
   b. Only borrow as a last resort.
   c. Tend to borrow from banks or other business sources.
   d. Ask friends and family because they know I'll pay.

10. When eating out with friends, I prefer to . . .
    a. Divide the bill proportionately.
    b. Ask for separate checks.
    c. Charge the bill to my credit/debit card and have others pay me.
    d. Pay the entire bill because I like to treat my friends.

11. When it comes to tipping, I . . .
    a. Sometimes do and sometimes don't.
    b. Just call me Scrooge.
    c. Resent it, but always tip the right amount.
    d. Tip generously because I like to be well thought of.

12. If I suddenly came into a lot of money, I . . .
    a. Wouldn't have to work.
    b. Wouldn't have to worry about the future.
    c. Could really build up my business.
    d. Would spend a lot on family and friends and enjoy time with them more.

13. When indecisive about a purchase, I often tell myself . . .
    a. It's only money.
    b. It's a bargain.
    c. It's a good investment.
    d. He/she will love it.

14. In our family . . .
    a. I do/will handle all the money and pay all the bills.
    b. My partner does/will take care of the finances.
    c. I do/will pay my bills and my partner will do the same.
    d. We do/will sit down together to pay bills.

Score: Tally your answers by the number of times you chose each letter.

a. _____   c. _____
b. _____   d. _____

To understand your results, see the explanation on the back of this page.

UNDERSTANDING THE RESULTS OF YOUR MONEY MOTIVATION QUIZ

Money means different things to different people based on a variety of factors, such as temperament and life experiences. Often the meaning of money and the way it motivates us is subtle and something we are not always aware of. This simple quiz is designed to give you an indication of how strongly you are influenced by the following money motivations: Freedom, Security, Power, and Love.

The key to your money motivation is reflected in the relative number of A, B, C, or D answers.

"A" answers indicate that money relates to Freedom. To you, money means having the freedom to do what you like.

"B" answers indicate that money relates to Security. You need to feel safe and secure, and you desire the stability and protection that money supposedly provides.

"C" answers indicate that money relates to Power. Personal success and control are important to you, and you appreciate the power money sometimes provides.

"D" answers indicate that money relates to Love. You like to use money to express love and build relationships.

One of the keys to managing money wisely is to understand our relationship to it. We hope this exercise gives you some helpful insights. You may wish to share your scores with your spouse or a friend and discuss whether their perceptions of your money motivations are consistent with your scores.

WORKSHEET #6: MONEY AUTOBIOGRAPHY

Often how we relate to our money and possessions is heavily influenced, positively or negatively, by our early life experiences and how money was handled in the households we grew up in. Taking time to reflect upon the following questions can make us aware of those influences and allow us to take steps to change any negative behaviors they may have fostered.

Your History with Money

1. How would you describe your life with money so far?
2. How was money handled in your family? Who was your family's Chief Financial Officer?
3. Would you call your family of origin rich, poor, or neither?
4. What did you think about money as a child?
5. Did you have an allowance? How did that affect your relationship to money?
6. When you were growing up, did your family talk about money?
7. Would you call your family generous? If so, where did they give money?
8. What messages did you receive about giving and saving money?
9. How was money tied to faith in your family?

Money in Your Current Life

1. Who are your current financial role models?
2. In your current family, who handles the money?
3. If you have children, do you discuss money issues with them?
4. What are your practices of generosity? Do you tithe?
5. Do you feel that money is abundant or scarce?
6. Do you feel like you can afford what your family needs?
7. How much money comes through your life in a year? ten years?
8. How is your relationship with money related to your relationship with God?

CHAPTER 1

All Manner of Good

Here's a scene from a sleepless night. Perhaps you're familiar with it. You lie in bed trying to think happy thoughts and instead you can't seem to shake thinking about . . . money. The thoughts are not happy thoughts. You think about paying the bills or managing the debt. You wonder what your relationship to money says about what sort of person you are and what you value. Old family attitudes toward money and cultural expectations are tied up in your thoughts about money. And even though many churches seem hesitant to talk about money as a spiritual matter, you sense that God is tied up in all this too.

If you've ever had such a night (or day), you've already taken a step toward peace of mind. You picked up this study. Congratulations for making it this far! The first step toward a healthy relationship with your finances is to push back the fears and to become a student. What are we studying? The practical steps to a kind of financial well-being that liberates us for a grace-filled, abundant life with God.

John Wesley, the principal founder of the Methodist movement in the eighteenth century, knew how important this conversation was for Christians. In his classic sermon on the topic, "The Use of Money," he lamented that the society he lived in talked about money frequently, but it was "not sufficiently considered by those whom God hath chosen out of the world." Part of a full Christian life, a life of holiness, was to continue growing in our employment of this gift. And Wesley did consider money a gift to be used for "all manner of good."

People of faith have always known that spiritual struggles accompany our discussions of money. We can see this in the many references that the Bible makes to the subject. Money may be a gift, but as 1 Timothy 6:10 famously notes, "The love of money is the root of all kinds of evil." The prophet Isaiah knew our temptation to misuse money on things that are not good for us: "Why spend money for what isn't food, / and your earnings for what doesn't satisfy?" (Isaiah 55:2).

Then there's Jesus. Jesus talked a *lot* about money. He was a companion to both the rich and the poor, and he challenged both to act on what was really important in their lives. He seemed to know our struggles with both the potential and the dangers of wealth, and he knew about putting it in a good perspective. "No one can serve two masters," he said. "Either you will hate the one and love the other, or you will be loyal to the one and have contempt for the other. You cannot serve God and wealth" (Matthew 6:24).

The principal danger of the love of money, even if we don't feel that we have much of it, is that it can make us forgetful—forgetful of who we are, of what our responsibilities to others are, and forgetful of God. That forgetfulness can lead us to misplaced trust. The writer of the Book of Hebrews knew that: "Your way of life should be free from the love of money, and you should be content with what you have. After all, he has said, *I will never leave you or abandon you*" (Hebrews 13:5).

So, let's start our journey here—putting our trust in God. With trust we may have fewer of those restless nights wondering about where it's all going to come from, because God is the creator of all things and the giver of every gift. God desires that we live in close relationship with God and each other. And God has provided all the resources we need to flourish, no matter our condition.

In this chapter, we'll explore the tensions in our relationship to money and begin to develop a plan that will help us see our financial well-being in the light of our spiritual health. We'll look at how the cultural messages around money can feed into distorted views about our financial goals and priorities. And we'll begin the journey to financial well-being by starting a plan that reflects God's intentions for our lives.

Activity: The Idols We Keep

Though money itself is not innately a bad thing, it can become an idol—even a rival god—in some people's lives. Has there ever been a time in your life when you felt money or possessions became an idol in your life? How did it affect you?

The reality of life is that every day we must make financial decisions—often they're relatively small ones, and sometimes they are big ones. Often we make those decisions, even the major life decisions such as where we work and where we live and who our friends are, strictly on a monetary basis rather than on the basis of prayerful consideration of where God would have us work and live. When we do that, money has become our idol—it has become a rival god in our lives. So, while this study is about how to practically manage your money, it is also about values and priorities, joy and well-being, and most importantly, how to manage your money and resources to honor the God who provides them.

What Our Consumer Culture Says About Money

Too often our consumer culture feeds us some really bad information about money and possessions. We encounter these myths many times a day in many different ways.

One myth suggests that things bring us happiness. This is probably the most powerful of the myths, and it is certainly what the advertising media would like us to believe. They scream: Buy me! Drink me! Wear me! Drive me! Put me in your hair! Do this and you'll be happy, popular, powerful, and utterly desirable! But if things really did bring this much happiness, America would be a deliriously happy nation because we have a lot of things. But statistics on depression, suicide, divorce, addiction, and a host of other negative indicators suggest that maybe we're not overall a happy nation.

So why, in face of the all the evidence to the contrary, do we tend to live our lives as though things we can buy really do bring happiness? Maybe we've heard this lie over and over and over until we've finally concluded, consciously or unconsciously, that it must be true.

A second myth is that debt is expected and unavoidable. The implication that often accompanies this myth is that there are really no negative consequences to debt. In reality, there are both serious economic and spiritual dangers to debt, which we'll explore in a later chapter. The Bible warns us to be cautious about debt (Romans 13:8, for example). The cautious debtor is one who seeks to avoid entering into debt, is careful and strategic when incurring debt, and always repays debt.

The last myth we'll explore is the one that tells us that a little more money will solve every problem. Some interesting research has been done related to this myth. People at various points along the economic continuum were asked how much more money they would need to really be "okay" financially. Here's the finding:

Whether they were making $25,000 or $250,000, the answer to how much more they needed was always right around 10 percent more. The truth is, if we haven't learned to handle well what we have, having more will leave us with the same set of problems, only bigger (apparently about 10 percent or so bigger!).

Activity: The Myths We Believe

1. Whether we're aware of it or not, we are constantly influenced by the culture we live in, and often that means we buy into these myths when it comes to money and possessions. Read the list below and put a check mark next to the myth that you think influences you the most.

   • Things bring us happiness.

   • Debt is expected and unavoidable.

   • A little more money will solve all my problems.

2. How has believing this myth influenced the way you live your life?

Money and the Faithful Way

How do we guard against being influenced by the myths of our consumer culture and controlled by this powerful force called *money*? By acknowledging and submitting ourselves to a more powerful force—the faithful way toward financial well-being.

While our consumer culture is hard at work trying to influence and control our financial behavior, God and the faithful way are quietly encouraging us to not be conformed to this world but to be transformed by the renewing of our minds. We renew our minds by understanding what the Bible says about money and our relationship to it. And the Bible has a great deal to say. In Scripture, we see three core truths about how God tells us to use our resources:

1. God created everything.

    Genesis 1 tells us that, in the beginning, there was nothing, and God created every grain of sand and every star in the universe. There was nothing, and then there was everything, all orchestrated by God alone.

2. God owns everything.

    God didn't create everything and then turn God's back on the creation. Scripture makes it clear that God continues to be involved and has retained ownership of all of creation: "The earth is the Lord's, and everything in it, / the world and its inhabitants too" (Psalm 24:1). The concept that God is the owner of everything may be easy to say, but it is often very hard to move that concept from our head to our hearts.

3. We are trustees, not the owners, of all God has made.

    If God created everything and retained ownership of everything, then we are trustees, not owners, of God's creation and resources. That's a powerful thought and an awesome privilege. But here's the key: First Corinthians 4:2 says, "In this kind of situation, what is expected of a manager is that they prove to be faithful."

So, in order to be faithful we must understand the role of a trustee. A trustee, while a privileged and trusted position, has responsibilities. The key responsibility is to care for and manage what belongs to someone else. For example, if someone became incapacitated and you were made trustee of his or her affairs, you would not own that person's assets, only the responsibility of handling them in accordance with the person's wishes and in the person's best interests.

The importance of our role as trustees can't be overemphasized. All other biblical financial principles flow out of this understanding. God has given us many and varied resources and these assets are part of how the work of God is done on earth. Our relationship to money changes when we keep in mind that we are handling the assets of God and are entrusted by God to make good choices.

Activity: Owner or Trustee?

Reflect on your own finances and possessions. Put an X on the continuum below to reflect how you see yourself, whether as an owner or a trustee.

I see myself as
an owner.

I see myself as
a trustee.

Repeat the activity while considering specific things: of my home, of my salary, of my time.

The Pull of the Consumer Culture vs. the Faithful Way

Foolish

Faithful

The Consumer Culture | The Faithful Way

Throughout this study, we will continue to talk about the pull of the consumer culture on us versus the faithful way toward financial well-being. The graphic above illustrates this tension, and you will see it appear throughout our study as a reminder of the battle we often face, specifically in this area of our finances. We are constantly asked to choose one way—the way that seems best to us or asking the Lord to lead us in all our decisions.

In a parable found in Luke 12:15-21, Jesus tells the story of the rich "fool":

Then Jesus said to them, "Watch out! Guard yourself against all kinds of greed. After all, one's life isn't determined by one's possessions, even when someone is very wealthy." Then he told them a parable: "A certain rich man's land produced a bountiful crop. He said to himself, What will I do? I have no place to store my harvest! Then he thought, Here's what I'll do. I'll tear down my barns and build bigger ones. That's where I'll store all my grain and goods. I'll say to myself, You have stored up plenty of goods, enough for several years. Take it easy! Eat, drink, and enjoy yourself. But God said to him, 'Fool, tonight you will die. Now who will get the things you have prepared for yourself?' This is the way it will be for those who hoard things for themselves and aren't rich toward God."

Luke 12:15-21

At first glance, we might not think the rich man's actions were foolish. After all, he's storing up his wealth and saving it, providing for his future. The problem is in his focus—he's concerned about his stuff and its protection more than he is about his responsibilities toward God and neighbor. John Wesley would have said that he was behaving more like a proprietor, one who has sole control over things, rather than a steward, who is entrusted with someone else's goods. In his sermon on "The Use of Money," Wesley said God "placed you here not as a proprietor, but a steward."

Maybe you see the "bigger barns" problem in our consumer culture today. Our houses are twice as big as they were sixty years ago. Our families are 25 percent smaller, but our closets, attics, basements, and garages are so full of stuff, that the self-storage business, which didn't even exist in 1960, is now a booming industry! Cultural messages may encourage us to hoard for ourselves, but Jesus called the rich man a "fool" for not being rich toward God.

The question raised by this parable is: How do we steward what has been entrusted to us in ways that reflect our faith in God? How can we be faithful and not foolish?

In this study, we will cover five areas of our financial lives:

- Earning
- Giving
- Saving
- Debt
- Spending

These areas represent the usual way we get money, through earning, and then the four things we can do with it once we have it: We can give it away, save it, pay debt with it, or spend it. How we allocate between these four uses is a function of just two things: Our prior commitments and our priorities and values.

Wesley reduced his beliefs about money to three simple rules: gain all you can, save all you can, and give all you can. As we flesh these out through this

> ## KEY QUESTION
>
> Will God consider my financial decisions to be faithful or foolish?

study, we will discover how Wesley saw these rules in the Bible and what it would mean for us to follow them. When those rules are applied to these five financial areas, we become:

- Diligent Earners
- Generous Givers
- Wise Savers
- Cautious Debtors
- Prudent Spenders

When we embrace these qualities and a faithful relationship with money, we become free of anxiety and can begin to achieve genuine financial well-being.

Activity: Faithful or Foolish?

1. Think about some of the financial decisions you've made over the last few days, large or small. Reflect for a few moments on whether you think God would consider them faithful or foolish and write your thoughts in the space below.

2. In which of the five financial areas listed on the previous page do you feel you need to grow? How might growth in that area lead you to be a faithful trustee of God's resources?

Why Create a Spending Plan?

When we talk about financial well-being, the key word we focus on is *contentment*. *Contentment* is not something that's related to a particular amount of money or circumstance, but it's an inward attitude, a serenity, that comes from doing the right and faithful thing and trusting in God to see it through. Ecclesiastes talks about the contentment of those who give themselves to diligent work rather than to concern over riches: "Sweet is the worker's sleep, whether there's a lot or a little to eat; but the excess of the wealthy won't let them sleep" (Ecclesiastes 5:12).

What we hope to show you throughout this study is that being financially faithful leads to being financially content. We can't know exactly how God will respond to every financial situation in our lives, but we do know that God honors our trusting and following God's principles.

We can work toward this sense of contentment and well-being by creating a customized Spending Plan to guide us. Some people call this a "budget." We know this word has negative connotations for some, but what we hope to do is give you a new perspective about this misunderstood tool. Money is a powerful thing. A budget, or a Spending Plan, is the fundamental tool that enables us to control our money so it doesn't control us.

A Spending Plan is a plan for how we will allocate our financial resources. Think about building a new house and installing the plumbing. We don't just run the main water line into our basement and let the water run wherever it wants to go—we have a plumbing plan to divert the water to where it's needed. But sometimes it seems we just let our income gush into our lives, with no plan on how to divert it into the areas that fulfill our goals. Whether it's a gush or a trickle, we want our financial resources to go to the right places and be used in ways that are consistent with our goals and are honoring to God.

We make plans in order to achieve a goal, and a Spending Plan is a way to reach our financial goals and live out our values and priorities. It's the means of achieving those goals you wrote out in your pre-work; and in turn, those goals help provide you with the motivation to stick to the plan when the going gets tough.

FINANCIAL WELL-BEING

The contentment we feel as we faithfully manage our financial resources according to God's principles and purposes.

THE SPENDING PLAN:

The fundamental tool that enables us to control our money so that it doesn't control us.

Again, throughout this process remind yourself that a Spending Plan is not meant to be restrictive or confining, but a tool that produces well-being. A foundational principle is that there is no true freedom without limits. A Spending Plan sets safe financial limits that allow you to reach a sense of well-being within those safe limits.

Imagine you're vacationing on a beautiful beach. A hundred yards or so out in the water, someone has set out some ropes and buoys. Beyond the ropes and buoys are dangerous undertows and shark activity, but within the ropes and buoys, you can swim and play in safety and with complete freedom. Of course you can swim beyond the buoys if you want, but it's not the smartest thing to do and could be very costly.

Now translate that image to thinking about a Spending Plan. A Spending Plan sets safe boundaries for how we use our money. By spending within its limits, we can safely and freely enjoy our resources. It's easy to spend beyond those limits, especially with credit cards. But if we do, we could easily get sucked down by the undertow of debt.

The hope of this study is for you to live in the well-being that comes from following the faithful way and using the resources God has entrusted to you for all manner of good to the best of your ability. We know this study can help you get there.

Activity: Wrapping It Up

- In this session, what new insights did you get into the role of money in our spiritual lives?

- How were your thoughts about a budget (a Spending Plan) changed by this session?

- What one word would you use to describe your relationship to your finances at this point?

- What are some specific things you hope to glean from this study?

CHAPTER 2

Getting Started:
Tracking Expenses and Income

I can still do anything I did at twenty," someone boasted on their fiftieth birthday. "I just need three days to recover." Most of us find that the older we get, the harder we have to work to maintain our health. Nutritional practices and exercises that once seemed optional now seem essential. If we are mindful, we discover things about our bodies and our limits that can help us feel much happier as we go about our lives. Though we have complaints, we understand that our bodies, these miraculous instruments, are gifts from God.

We can have a similar experience with money. For some of us, thinking about our financial lives is something like an unpleasant necessity we have to deal with from time to time. *How wonderful it would be*, we might think, *if I made just enough money not to have to think about it.*

Your Money Autobiography may have revealed that you grew up in an environment where money was something that you didn't discuss in polite company or in church. Maybe it wasn't even talked about in your home. If you didn't get verbal messages about money, you surely picked up on what wasn't said. And when you got your own income and bills, you started developing habits that were based on the beliefs about money that you pieced together from all these messages.

Just as with health, being mindful about finances allows you to live a happier life. Trying not to think about this area of life is not happiness. In fact, it can bring a host of anxieties. But learning about finances and beginning practices that increase our financial well-being actually is liberating.

Like Jesus (who, remember, talked a *lot* about money), John Wesley was aware of how money impacts our souls and our relationship to God. You might be surprised to hear that the first of Wesley's simple rules on the use of money was: Gain all you can. After all, if the love of money is the root of all evil (1 Timothy 6:10), wouldn't having more money tempt us to love it more?

Wesley added a lot of qualifications to that general rule. He did not advise people to gain money at the cost of their minds, their lives, their health, or through harm to their neighbors. But he did see the importance of "honest industry," or giving your best to the work in which you are employed and earning money through that work. Wesley was a great fan of the biblical phrase, "Whatever you are capable of doing, do with all your might" (Ecclesiastes 9:10).

Where he differed from the culture around him was in the *purpose* for earning. Christians were not to accumulate wealth (like the foolish barn builder we met in chapter 1) simply to create comfort for themselves. They also don't gain all they can just so that they don't have to think about money. Wesley believed that money was a gift, like our bodily health, that we can steward in ways that give glory to God. In our earning, as in our giving, we can become more fully alive and more fully aware of the abundant life God intends for all people.

So what we need are some tools and practices that will help us understand our financial health. When our financial picture is mysterious, we aren't able to connect our finances with our faith in a clear way. We're also prone to all sorts of anxieties and fears about the future.

On the other hand, with a clear picture we can begin to make some decisions that are connected to our values and to God's intentions for us. The steps may seem small at first, but each one moves us to a greater sense of well-being and openness to God.

In this chapter, we'll get some of those tools and start on those practices that will lead us to more mindful living as it relates to our finances. We will also keep growing in our knowledge of God and the faithful way toward financial well-being. In all this we will discover new dimensions of what Jesus means by saying, "I came so that they could have life—indeed, so that they could live life to the fullest" (John 10:10).

Activity: Getting Started

What are some ways the "pull of the consumer culture" regarding money or possessions impacted you this week?

At the end of our last chapter, we talked about how creating and following a Spending Plan protects us and allows us to experience financial well-being. In this chapter, we will dive into the first steps of creating a Spending Plan.

A Spending Plan is important because it allows us to face our finances with a healthy dose of reality. Though it may be hard to take an honest look at our financial reality, doing so can actually remove the uncertainty and anxiety we feel when we don't know the true situation. In fact, facing that reality, having a plan, and seeing where our money is going actually does more than just remove uncertainty and anxiety—it can prevent a lot of future regret.

Another benefit of a Spending Plan is that it helps avoid waste. Without a Spending Plan, we are apt to spend more money, and that might mean we waste some of the resources that God has entrusted to us. A Spending Plan helps keep these values and priorities in the forefront of our minds and lives, helping us reflect what is really important to us. Without it, we can easily fall into spending patterns that don't reflect our faith in God and conflict with our financial goals. Following a Spending Plan ensures that our walk will be consistent with our talk.

Finally, as we've said before, having a Spending Plan leads to financial well-being. A Spending Plan enables us to spend with confidence and freedom because it sets up those safe limits we talked about. Going out to dinner knowing that we are within our safe spending boundaries is much more enjoyable than going out wondering how we're going to pay for it, or whether it will add to our credit card debt. That sense of safety and well-being trickles down and gets experienced by your family members as well. Children can sense financial tension, and that tension can shape their perspective on money down the road. It is important to model and talk about healthy habits for our children.

A Spending Plan benefits everyone—at all points along the economic continuum—and not just for people in financial difficulty, as we often believe.

Activity: Benefits of a Spending Plan

Take a moment and put a check mark by the benefit listed in the sidebar that you think will most impact your life. What are a few reasons why you think this will help or what do you hope to gain in that area?

Activity: My Goals

On page 166 of this workbook, you will find a blank Spending Plan form. This is the master plan that you will be using throughout this study. If you need an additional copy of this form, you can download a copy at abingdonpress.com/savinggrace. Other worksheets and forms, including versions that will do the calculations for you, can be found there in PDF formats.

THE **BENEFITS** OF A SPENDING PLAN

- Allows us to face reality.
- Avoids waste.
- Keeps our values and priorities in the forefront.
- Leads to financial well-being.

You'll notice that the Spending Plan looks a lot like the "What I Spend" sheet you filled out in your pre-work. The pre-work sheet was used to illustrate what you currently spend, and the goal of this study is to convert what you currently spend into a Spending Plan that better reflects your goals—to move from "what is" to "what I want it to be."

Refer back to your pre-work and the "Goals to Achieve This Year." Your goals are key to this process, and each category of your Spending Plan should reflect those goals. Your goals will be the ongoing motivators for sticking to the plan when the going gets a little tough.

Take just a moment to pause and revisit the goals you came up with in your pre-work. Do they accurately reflect where you want to be in your financial life? Do you need to make any changes?

Prioritize your goals, and list the top three in the space provided:

Goal 1:

Goal 2:

Goal 3:

Track Your Expenses

Now that you've thought about the Spending Plan and prioritized your financial goals, the next step is to track where your money is going. For many people, this is a frustrating part of the budgeting process; but tracking expenses is simpler than it seems, takes less time than you think, and it doesn't require an advanced degree in math. You can begin immediately using a simple record-keeping system to track where your money is currently going.

On the next page is a form titled "Spending Record Example."

Side 1 of the form appears on page 32 and lists the monthly variable expenses. These are the categories in which you don't spend the same amount of money every month. These are also generally the hardest-to-control categories when it comes to spending. Once you have completed your master Spending Plan, you will use line (1) of the form to list the amount of money you plan to dedicate to each category per month. For example, in this form we have listed a goal of $200 per month for gas. As the month progressed, we made gas purchases in the amounts of $64, $42, $38, and $58. Our total for the month was $202, which was $2 over our Spending Plan goal for the month.

SPENDING RECORD EXAMPLE

Daily Variable Expenses

	Transportation		Household						Professional Services	Entertainment		
	Gas, etc.	Maint./Repair	Groceries	Clothes	Gifts	Household Items	Personal	Other		Going Out	Travel	Other
(1) Spending Plan	200	40	480	150	80	75	50	---	---	100	70	40
	64	21	186	89	17	14	16	25		22	70	22 (sitter)
	42		22	46	55	22	18			46		
	38		20	50		9				19		
	85		172			31						
			18									
			8									
			20									
(2) Total	202	21	446	185	72	76	34	25	---	87	70	22
(3) Over/Under	(2)	19	34	(35)	8	(1)	16	(25)	---	13	---	18
(4) Last Mo. YTD												
(5) This Mo. YTD												

X̶ X̶ X̶ X̶ X̶ X̶ X̶ X̶ X̶ 1̶0̶ 1̶1̶ 1̶2̶ 1̶3̶ 1̶4̶ 1̶5̶ 1̶6̶ 1̶7̶ 1̶8̶ 1̶9̶ 2̶0̶ 2̶1̶ 2̶2̶ 2̶3̶ 2̶4̶ 2̶5̶ 2̶6̶ 2̶7̶ 2̶8̶ 2̶9̶ 3̶0̶ 3̶1̶

- Use this page to record expenses that tend to be daily, variable expenses—often the hardest to control.
- Keep receipts throughout the day and record them at the end of each day.
- Total each category at the end of the month (line 2) and compare to the Spending Plan (line 1). Subtracting line 2 from line 1 gives you an (over) or under the budget figure for that month (line 3).
- To verify that you have made each day's entry, cross out the number at the bottom of the page that corresponds to that day's date.
- Optional: If you wish to monitor your progress as you go through the year, you can keep cumulative totals in lines 4 and 5.

SPENDING RECORD EXAMPLE

MONTH: _January_

Monthly Regular Expenses (generally paid by check once a month)

	Giving		Savings	Debt			Housing				Auto Payments	Insurance		Misc. Cash Expenses
	Church	Other		Credit Cards	Education	Other	Mortgage/Rent	Maintenance	Utilities	Other		Auto/Home	Life/Medical	
(1) Spending Plan	280	30	155	75	50	---	970	30	180	25	350	90	40	65
	140	20	155	75	50		970		95 (elec)	44	350		40	65
	140	10	200						31 (gas)					
									79 (tel)					
(2) Total	280	30	355	75	50	---	970	---	205	44	350	---	40	65
(3) (Over)/Under	---	---	(200)	---	---	---	---	30	(25)	(19)	---	90	---	---
(4) Last Mo. YTD														
(5) This Mo. YTD														

- This page allows you to record major monthly expenses for which you typically write just one or two checks per month.
- Entries can be recorded as the checks are written (preferably) or by referring back to the check ledger at a convenient time.
- Total each category at the end of the month (line 2) and compare to the Spending Plan (line 1). Subtracting line 2 from line 1 gives you an (over) or under the budget figure for that month (line 3).
- Use the "Monthly Assessment" section to reflect on the future actions that will be helpful in staying on course.

MONTHLY ASSESSMENT

Area	(Over)/Under	Reason	Future Action
Clothes	(35)	After-Christmas Sales	No new clothes next month
Savings	(200)	Gift from Aunt Mary	N/A
Utilities	(25)	Electricity and phone	check phone plan
Insurance	90	Quarterly bill next month	N/A

Areas of Victory   _Feels great to be ahead on savings. Thanks, Aunt Mary!_
I'm really proud of how we're doing!

Areas to Watch   _Need to look hard at ways to save on electricity and phone bills._

On the second page of the form, you will see where to track your regular monthly expenses. This is where you record the bills you normally pay once a month that are usually fixed amounts. These expenses are typically easier to control since they don't change often.

Once you start tracking these expenses over the next few weeks, you will have valuable information about how much you're spending in each category and a better idea of what amounts you need to plug into your master Spending Plan.

Here's the plan to start tracking your expenses today:

1. Save your receipts.

   Save every receipt. It helps to keep these in a consistent place as you make daily purchases. That can be your left-hand pants pocket or a certain section of your purse, or even a folder on your computer, or a special envelope labeled "receipts." For online purchases, take a screenshot of the invoice or receipt (any screen with the name of the vendor, the date, and the purchase amount) and keep those images in a dedicated folder on your computer or phone. You will need the receipts to categorize the expenses. For example, a trip to Target could involve purchases for clothing, household, and food. You'll want to review that receipt, because tracking expenditures online just tells you the total you spent at Target—not what those expenditures were for.

2. Record your purchases every day.

   With your receipts in tow, at the end of the day, record the amount of each receipt under the proper categories. There are two ways you can do that. One is to just write it down on the form. Most people find it easier and faster for this first month to use the pencil-and-paper method. At the bottom of the paper form, you will see numbers listed for each day of the month. These days can be marked through as you record that day's expenses. If you prefer, you can use a digital version of a spending record. An advantage of using it is that it automatically shows total expenditures to date for each category. But if you use the digital form, still be sure to enter your expenditures each day.

A few hints for making this record-keeping process a little easier: First, if you're using the paper form, keep it where you will see it and record on it daily—don't tuck it away in a drawer. If you use the digital version, put it on your daily to-do list or set a reminder on your phone or calendar. Another tip is to round off your purchases to the nearest dollar for simplicity. Also, feel free to combine or rename categories to better fit your expenses and lifestyle. For example, you may want to add a category for Takeout Food if you frequently order in, or if ordering in has become a problematic part of your budget!

Finally, remember to assign sales tax amounts proportionally to the appropriate categories. (See more about this on the next page as we break down an example of a day's worth of receipts.)

3. Create a miscellaneous Small Cash category.

Another way to simplify is to add a miscellaneous Small Cash category to your form. Determine an amount of money each month for little items like drinks, snacks, or other small purchases, and carry that amount of cash with you in an envelope or a special place in your wallet. In doing so, you don't have to record every small purchase you make each day, and it will help to keep spending on those items within your Spending Plan allocation. For example, if your monthly Small Cash allocation is $40, and your average expenditure is $2, you will save making twenty entries per month.

This is also a great way to get a reality check on how small purchases tend to add up to more than you think. When you run out of the money you set aside for these items by the tenth of the month, you can see how those expenses are accumulating.

> ## HINTS FOR **TRACKING YOUR EXPENSES**
>
> - Keep your Spending Record Form where you will see and record on it daily.
> - Round off to the nearest dollar.
> - Combine or rename categories if necessary.
> - Have a miscellaneous Small Cash category for small expenditures.
> - Remember to assign sales tax proportionally to the appropriate categories.

Then you can decide whether to increase the money in the category or make an effort to cut back.

Activity: Recording Receipts

Let's assume it's the end of the day, and you've made some purchases. Make a copy of the Spending Record form on page 167 to use for this activity. You will need it to record the transactions below. You may also want to make a few additional copies to have on hand to use as you begin tracking your own spending.

Note: If you need additional copies or if you would prefer a PDF where the calculations are done for you, you can find them at abingdonpress.com/savinggrace.

Below is a list of your purchases for the day:

- A Main Street Gas receipt for $52

- A paint store receipt for $38

- A Neighborhood Foods receipt for $77

- You have a department store receipt that is a little more complicated. It contains items that should go in two different categories. The receipt also has almost $10 in sales tax that needs to be allocated. The items are a knit jacket at $69 and a king-size linen sheet for $41. Split the sales tax proportionally between your two purchases. (Estimating is fine, so when tracking your own expenses, you might choose to break the tax up a bit differently).

- There is another receipt for the lunch you had with a friend where you picked up the tab. Her lunch was $14.97 while your meal was $12.48. Your tax was $2.40, and your tip was $6.00. You have flexibility where to record this receipt. Maybe it's under Going Out, or under Gifts if it was a birthday lunch for your friend, or maybe under Entertainment "Other." The key is to be consistent over time as to where you put such expenditures.

- Finally, you have a receipt for about $1.00 that you spent on a soft drink. Well, it could go in a category, or you could have used your miscellaneous Small Cash fund for that purpose. You don't need to allocate it at all.

This exercise probably only took you a few minutes to complete but accomplished a lot in terms of you understanding where your money is going. Not only will those couple of minutes ensure that you have the information you need

KEY QUESTION

Is it worth two minutes a day of record keeping to bring this crucial area of my life—my spending—under control?

for future wise decisions, but the simple act of recording expenses will have a strong influence on your spending behavior. You will be giving yourself daily feedback on what is actually taking place, and that will be a strong source of encouragement and correction in this process.

Activity: Which Form Will You Use?

1. Before we move on, take a minute to decide if you're going to use the pencil-and-paper form or a digital form for your record keeping over the next month, and write your decision below.

   I will use the _____ form.

2. If you are using the written form, decide where you will keep it so that it's handy, and record your decision below.

   I will keep the written form _____so I will see it daily.

3. If you are using the digital form, think about how you will remind your-self to enter your receipts daily.

   I will _____.

Track Your Income

An important step in developing your Spending Plan is to consider your income, or what you earn. Earning is about more than just getting money—it's also an opportunity to consider the tension we face between choosing to follow the pull of the consumer culture or seeking the faithful way to financial well-being.

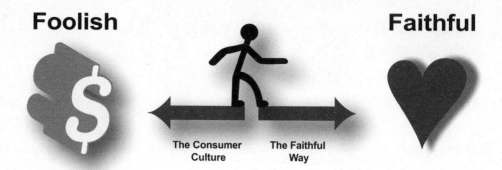

Foolish

Faithful

The Consumer Culture

The Faithful Way

The pull of the consumer culture says, "Your value is measured by your position, your paycheck, the car you drive or the house you live in." It drives us to earn more, tries to convince us to become workaholics, and deceives us with the myth, "A little more money will solve all my problems."

When we explore the faithful way, we find a very different message. The Creation story in Genesis 1 tells us that humans are made in the image of God, and it is that basic relationship with God that determines our value—not what we earn or what we do. Scripture makes it clear that work is a blessing. After creating human beings and breathing life into them, God placed them in a garden and gave them a role to fulfill. They were to cultivate and keep the garden as co-creators with God. In our work to improve and manage the resources God created, we get to participate in God's ongoing work and our own work has dignity and worth (Genesis 1–2).

We've strayed from that view of work and often see work as a curse rather than a blessing. Since our jobs are where many of us spend a majority of our waking hours, it can and should serve as a key place where we have the opportunity to flourish and exercise our faith.

The Bible characterizes the earner who honors God as "diligent." We define the Diligent Earner as one who works with commitment, purpose, and a grateful attitude. In Colossians 3:23, the apostle Paul writes, "Whatever you do, do it from

WHAT OUR CONSUMER CULTURE SAYS ABOUT EARNING

- Your value is measured by your position, your paycheck, the kind of car you drive, or the house you live in.
- A little more money will solve all your problems.

the heart for the Lord and not for people." God invites us to purposeful work. We should work as though we are working for the Lord rather than for people. It's God who gave us our minds and bodies to do our work. Seeing the world and our place in it through the lens of God's intentions helps us see our income and our earning in a whole new light.

Your Spending Plan: Income

Net Take-Home Pay

Turn now to your master Spending Plan. Notice under Salary #1 and #2, you are to put down net take-home pay. That is the amount of your paycheck after all taxes and deductions. That is the amount of money you have to manage.

While we are only going to deal with net take-home pay, you also need to be aware of and review the deductions from your paycheck. For example: a large tax refund means more than necessary was withheld for federal taxes, so the government had free use of your money for the last year. If this is true, you may want to adjust your withholdings. An online calculator to help you determine the appropriate amount to be withheld is available at www.irs.gov (search for "withholding calculator").

Also, be sure you are on the most cost-effective health insurance plan for your situation. Also, consider taking advantage of a Flex Spending Plan or Health Savings Account for dependent care or additional medical expenses. If your employer offers a matching funds program for retirement savings, be sure to contribute to the plan to take advantage of that free money.

Variable Income

The net take-home figure is an easy figure to work with if your paycheck stays the same every pay period. But what if you have variable income, such as someone who is self-employed or on commission? Budgeting becomes more complicated when you don't know how much you are

> ## EARNING AND THE FAITHFUL WAY
>
> - Our value is not measured by what we earn or do, but by who we are: beloved [children] of God, created in the image of God (Genesis 1:27).
> - We are called to work with commitment, purpose, and a grateful attitude (Colossians 3:23).

bringing home every month. Many people assume that if your income is variable, you can't really budget. This is not the case. The answer is to take a conservative estimate of your after-tax annual income—based on your income over the past few years (if you've been in the job for a while)—and then divide that figure by twelve. For example: $36,000 net annual income divided by twelve results in an estimated average income of $3,000 per month. That's your monthly budgeted figure in this example.

> ## NET **TAKE-HOME** PAY:
> - The amount of the paycheck after all taxes and deductions.

But what if you have a good month and bring in $3,500? What do you do with the extra $500? Well, that $500 isn't really extra. As your income is variable, you may need it next month if you don't reach the $3,000 average you have budgeted. Put that $500 in savings and live on the $3,000 according to your Spending Plan. If the next month's commissions fall short, you draw on the saved amount to once again have $3,000 for your Spending Plan.

Another key point if you're self-employed: be sure you are setting money aside for quarterly taxes. (There's more information on variable incomes and how to arrive at a conservative estimate in the appendix. See "Determining an Average Month for Variable Income" on page 131.)

Two Incomes

Many households today have two incomes. It's not feasible for everyone, but you might ask, are we able to live on only one income? Could we give a portion, save a portion, and cover all the basic necessities (such as food, clothing, housing, transportation, debt, or retirement) with one income? The obvious advantage of this is that, should you lose one income for any reason, your basic needs can still be met with one income. If you can, consider putting your second income into savings and using it only for extras, like accelerated debt repayment, above-and-beyond giving, special travel and entertainment, additional savings, or any other nonessentials. That plan won't work for everyone, but it's certainly worth considering.

Raises

What if you earn a raise? Maybe you're the type of person who naturally says 10 percent of the raise goes to giving to God's work and 10 percent goes to savings. But even those who tithe and are disciplined savers would have to admit that the other 80 percent of that new income is likely to disappear into a black hole. Spending tends to rise with our income, and soon enough, most of us can't tell where our raises went.

Yet raises can add up to a significant amount of additional income in just a few years' time. For example, a 4 percent raise each year over a short three-year period results in additional cumulative gross income during that period of almost 25 percent of the original salary. (The math that backs up that statement appears on page 132 in your appendix, "What Happens to Your Raises?")

When John Wesley was a student at Oxford, he lived on twenty-eight pounds a year. Throughout his life as his income grew, he continued to live on that same twenty-eight pounds. By living below his means and not incorporating his raises into his day-to-day life, Wesley was able to dedicate more and more to his discipline of giving and saving.

Here's the point: whatever your financial goals are, deciding ahead of time how to use raises or any unexpected income, can be an important strategy in reaching your financial goals. The key question is: How will you allocate any new income?

Activity: Allocating New Income

What will you do with your next raise or any other unexpected income? Below, record how you will allocate that income and apply it to your goals.

Any raises or unexpected income will be allocated toward:

MY SPENDING PLAN: INCOME

Fill in your net income in the Income category on your master Spending Plan form. (Since in all likelihood your income hasn't changed since you did your pre-work, you can probably copy it from your What I Spend pre-work form.)

Congratulations! You've just completed the first section of your Spending Plan.

If you need an additional copy of this form or any other form or worksheet, you can download a copy at abingdonpress.com /savinggrace. A digital PDF version of the form that will perform the calculations is also available.

Activity: Wrapping Up

1. Considering your work life, are there any adjustments you might want or need to make in order to be more in line with the faithful way toward your work?

   My thoughts:

2. Begin or continue recording your daily expenses using the Spending Record Form provided.

Setting Up Your Finances with Your Congregation

Now that we've begun talking about an approach to financial freedom that liberates us to trust and serve God, let's explore what that means for you as a minister. In these special clergy-focused sections, we're going to talk about some of the unique features of clergy finances and the role that you play in helping others live into financial health and well-being. We're also going to confront some of the thought-processes and barriers that keep us from being the financial leaders we can be. In addition to these sections of the clergy workbook, you will also find free videos featuring Phil and Janet Jamieson on Amplify Media. To view the videos, visit AmplifyMedia.com and search Saving Grace (these videos are also included on the *Saving Grace* DVD). These videos provide helpful recaps of the material in these sessions and can be a great way to begin small group sessions discussing this material.

Nothing quite prepares you for the many decisions you need to make as a clergyperson entering ministry. Because of the way clergy are treated in the U.S. tax code, clergy have a bewildering array of terms that often seem to overlap in meaning and that have varying impacts on your short- and long-term future. In The United Methodist Church, pastors must make important decisions about their finances in conversation with the local church they serve, with some items requiring action by a charge conference.

> **CLERGY VIDEOS**
>
> Videos for the clergy sessions are available at AmplifyMedia.com (search Saving Grace) and are included on the *Saving Grace* DVD.

In this chapter we will give you some of the definitions and tools you need to approach these decisions with more confidence. The terrain for clergy finances shifts frequently, so it will be important for you to monitor tax laws and changes in your denomination's pension and benefit plans. Many clergy will rely on the assistance of a tax professional and financial advisor to help them navigate this changing landscape. The good news is that there are a number of features in the tax code that can benefit clergy.

Even if you have been in your current position for a while, this chapter will be of interest to you. Each year, United Methodist clergy are asked to work with their church to create a clergy compensation form for the coming year. You can begin planning now for the next time you have that conversation with your Staff/Pastor-Parish Relations Committee or the equivalent body in your church.

Debt

Part of the backdrop of any discussion of personal finances is debt. In other parts of this workbook, there are sections and exercises to help you address types of debt that affect many people, not just clergy. Consumer debt, home mortgages, and the realities of everyday life create liabilities that need to be accounted for in any personal budget. Looking at your compensation in light of those obligations is important.

There is one form of debt, however, that creates a particular pressure for many clergy as they enter their early years of ministerial service—educational debt. Many denominations, including The United Methodist Church, require a seminary-level master's degree for clergy seeking ordination. Added to the cost of an undergraduate degree, the tuition and fees related to preparation for ministry can prompt many students to take on a significant debt load to complete their education. A 2015 *Christian Century* article noted that the average debt for theological students at graduation is close to $40,000. That level of debt is sobering when you consider that it is almost at the level of the annual median wage for clergy.

If you are still a student, it pays to take stock of your resources for funding your education that might keep you from taking out an excessive amount of student loans. Spend some time with the staff in your school's financial aid office to explore the range of aid packages and scholarships that may be available to you. Consider work-study programs that could reduce your tuition payments.

Talk with your denomination's staff about scholarships and grants available through their offices. In The United Methodist Church, these are administered by the General Board of Higher Education and Ministry. Some annual conferences in The UMC also offer service loans that can be repaid through years of ministerial service in the conference.

Don't be bashful about approaching your local church as well. Churches usually find that their own sense of vocation is renewed when they support new candidates for ministry. Let them partner with you to help fund your education. You may discover that it builds a holy and meaningful relationship for both of you.

If you have already graduated, the information found in other parts of this book will be helpful to you in addressing the remaining balance on your loan. As with consumer debt, educational debt can cripple your sense of financial freedom if you let it linger. Early in your career, you will have competing demands for your limited resources and you will want to look at the retirement of your educational debt in light of those demands, but develop a plan to erase your debt as quickly as possible. Talk with a financial advisor about possibilities for loan consolidation and income-based repayment plans, if necessary, but make sure you are not limited in paying them off early.

Income: Determining Clergy Status

The first step in thinking about clergy compensation is determining if you are clergy. That may sound like a simple question, but the Internal Revenue Service (IRS) has two qualifications to be considered clergy that may differ from the standards of your denomination. Filing taxes as a clergyperson carries with it a number of uncommon tax provisions.

One requirement is that an individual must qualify as a "minister of the gospel," a definition about which the IRS generally allows some latitude. Most denominations and churches have a defined process for ordaining, commissioning, and licensing ministers. In The United Methodist Church, elders and deacons are ordained, provisional elders and deacons are commissioned, and local pastors are licensed for ministry. While these different statuses refer to varying roles within the denomination, for IRS purposes they are all considered to carry a "clergy" status.

However, in addition to this qualification, the IRS also requires that the individual be performing services that constitute ministerial duties. The person must perform some or all of these functions:

- administering sacerdotal functions (e.g., marriage and funeral services, baptisms, and Communion);
- considered to be a religious leader by a church or denomination;
- conducting religious worship;
- exercising management responsibility in the conduct of your church or denomination.

For most local church pastors, these are regular functions of your office. However, if you are in an extension ministry that does not involve these duties, or your role in the local church does not involve leadership of worship or managing the church, you will need to examine your tax status more closely and discuss it with your employer. Persons involved in the administration of a religious denomination or a church-related institution are generally considered to meet the qualifications, but there are IRS criteria to determine if an institution meets the threshold of being an integral part of the church with meaningful church control.

Salary

If you have determined that you can be considered "clergy" for tax purposes, you have unique tax circumstances related to the concept of "employment." At the federal level, there are two types of taxes that clergy pay when they file with IRS each year—income tax and social security tax. States also impose a variety of taxes, but we will only be dealing with federal taxes here. Be sure you understand the tax requirements of your state and the impact they may have on you as a clergyperson.

Income Tax—Most clergy are considered employees

On the income tax side, most ministers are considered to be employees of the church they serve. Pastors will generally receive a W-2 form every year from their church or charge. United Methodist elders, deacons, and licensed local pastors under appointment to a local church should receive a W-2 from that church even though their membership is with the annual conference and they are appointed by the bishop. Pastors should receive a W-2 even though, as we shall see, they are considered self-employed for Social Security.

Some clergy may also wonder why they are considered employed if their accountability structure allows them considerable freedom to determine what to do day-to-day. The IRS standard is that a minister is considered an employee if there is significant behavioral and financial control by the employer and the relationship between the church and the minister is in an ongoing, on-site relationship with the church that could be terminated.

Social Security Tax—Ministers are self-employed

With regard to Social Security taxes, which the clergyperson must also file each year, ministers in active service are treated as self-employed. The consequence of this determination is that ministers have to calculate Social Security tax on Schedule SE and report and pay the tax with Form 1040, the normal form for filing your income taxes. Ministers will pay the Social Security tax, along with their income taxes, through the year. They may do this by filing estimated taxes quarterly or by having the amount withheld by the church. If you do not pay quarterly by the IRS deadlines, you will be subject to penalties. Also, if you fail to correctly estimate your taxes, you may also have to pay penalties.

There are significant implications to this status. For instance, if a minister were not self-employed, the church would be obligated to deduct Social Security tax from the pastor's salary under the Federal Insurance Contributions Act (FICA). Self-employed individuals pay Social Security tax under the Self-Employment Contributions Act (SECA). Therefore, a church should not withhold FICA from a minister's paycheck.

It is possible for a minister to be exempt from SECA tax, but the consequences are stark. A minister must have a conscientious objection to receiving public insurance in order to claim an exemption. This also means that the minister would not be entitled to receive any Social Security benefits, which is a key part of many people's retirement planning.

Elements of Pastoral Compensation

As you meet with the body in your church that develops the clergy compensation package (in The United Methodist Church this is usually the Staff/Pastor-Parish Relations Committee), you will need to think about your salary in light of the tax significance discussed above. Two items in particular have tax implications that will be affected by how you and your congregation deal with them—accountable reimbursement (which is not actually compensation but church expenses paid by the clergyperson) and the housing allowance. Both of these are dealt with in the sections below.

Clergy Housing

As a clergyperson, your housing can provide you with a significant tax benefit. Whether the church provides you with housing (in the form of a parsonage) or you own or rent your own house, as a qualified minister you can receive a housing allowance that is excluded from income tax liability. You should plan with your church to properly designate this amount and to set an appropriate amount for the allowance.

Many people have the misperception that, by setting a housing allowance, the church is increasing the church's budget and payment to their clergyperson. This is not the case. The housing allowance is a portion of the pastor's compensation that is designated ahead of time as a housing allowance. For instance, a pastor with a total compensation of $60,000 per year might designate $20,000 of that amount as a housing allowance. The church would still be paying $60,000, but the amount of the pastor's taxable income could be $40,000 depending on their qualifying expenses related to housing.

It is important to note in all cases that this exclusion of a portion of income for housing-related expenses is only for income tax purposes. Clergy must still include the amount for their self-employment Social Security tax.

If a pastor lives in church-owned housing, the allowance for housing-related expenses is often called a parsonage allowance. Pastors may exclude expenses such as utilities, landscaping, furnishings, and property and casualty insurance (renter's insurance) as part of this allowance. It is important to carefully estimate these expenses when determining the amount of the allowance, and to track the expenses through the year. If the actual expenses amount to less than the parsonage allowance, the unused balance becomes taxable income. Also, expenses beyond the amount of the allowance will also be taxable.

The situation for pastors who own or rent their home is similar. However, in addition to the types of expenses listed above, other expenses are applicable to the exclusion, such as mortgage payments, real property taxes, and homeowner's association dues.

Whether the housing allowance is for a home provided by the church or for housing the minister provides, the amount that can be excluded from taxable income is dependent on other figures. The housing exclusion claimed by a minister cannot exceed any of these three amounts (in other words, the exclusion must be the smallest of the three):

- the actual amount spent from the minister's income on allowable expenses related to the home;
- the amount designated by the church for a housing allowance;
- the fair rental value of the home, including utilities and furnishings.

The first two factors are easily determined. The third requires some investigation by the pastor. Fair rental value is based on the rental value of similar residences in your area that are furnished in a comparable manner. You can determine that value based on your own determination, but you may want to enlist a local realtor to help.

In order to be properly designated, the housing or parsonage allowance must be approved by the church prior to the period in which the expenses will be incurred. In The United Methodist Church, the annual charge conference is usually the body that adopts the allowance for the subsequent year, identifying in writing the amount of the allowance and recording the action in its minutes. You should keep a copy of this written action of the church in your tax records.

You should make sure that the amount of this allowance accords with your estimated actual expenses, although some planners recommend that this should be the highest of the three factors, with any unused funds being brought back into tax calculations for income as unused housing. Remember that if an unanticipated expense occurs that would take you over the set allowance, the allowance cannot be changed. This is particularly important to communicate with your church at the time of a pastoral transition, since your expenses may differ from those of your predecessor.

It's also important to recognize that, while the fair rental value of a parsonage that is provided to a minister is not taxable for income tax purposes, it is for Social Security tax.

Accountable Reimbursement for Church Expenses

Another important area to discuss with your church is the method for reimbursing expenses related to your ministry. It is almost always more advantageous for a minister to have an accountable reimbursement plan with the church to cover these expenses. The IRS has certain requirements for such plans, and most annual conferences assist churches in adopting one at each annual charge conference.

You incur many expenses on behalf of the church in the course of ministry. Auto-related expenses are a major category for most pastors, but there are also expenses related to continuing education, professional subscriptions, vestments, and meals with parishioners. The standard for determining if an expense is reimbursable is that it must be both ordinary and necessary for the church. If the expense is one that is common and generally accepted in your field, it probably qualifies as ordinary. If it aids you in the pursuit of your work on behalf of the church, it should qualify as necessary. Personal expenses are not reimbursable. If you receive such a reimbursement it should be reported on your W-2 since it is taxable income.

The accountable part of a plan involves records you keep and submit to the church within a reasonable time frame for reimbursement. Those records should note the purpose of the expense and a mileage record and/or receipts to substantiate the expense. This type of documentation should be submitted regularly throughout the year. In general, every expense should be submitted within sixty days of the date it was incurred.

The pastor may find it is useful to submit expenses on two forms. A cash expense form, on which the date and business purpose of each expense can be recorded, should be accompanied by the receipts related to those expenses. The second form is a mileage log, on which you can document dates, destinations, and business purposes of trips.

If you are driving your own vehicle in the course of your work conducting church business, you may use one of two methods to determine expenses that are reimbursable. The standard mileage rate method uses a rate per mile determined by the government to estimate the average cost of operating an automobile. In 2020, that rate is 57.5 cents per mile. Many ministers prefer the simplicity of this method, and, with current mileage rates and costs, using the mileage rate is more advantageous. An accountable reimbursement plan with the church can set the reimbursement of mileage at this rate.

The alternative is an actual expense method in which the minister deter- mines the portion of fuel and maintenance costs related to business-related travel. This method may result in tax benefits if your operating costs exceed those allowed by the standard mileage rate method. It does, however, depend on more stringent record keeping that involves tracking depreciation of a vehicle.

Whatever method you choose, it is helpful to have a good estimate of your reimbursable expenses as you prepare your compensation for the coming year. As the pastor, you will often have great say in setting the amount of an accountable reimbursable plan. If properly documented and administered, these funds will not be taxable income and will not be reported to the IRS.

However, if you do not incur expenses up to the amount set in the agree- ment, you cannot receive the excess funds as income, at least not without pay- ing taxes on it. If the balance is given to you as a bonus, all the payments made for expenses during the whole year become taxable.

Some churches may offer expense allowances that are nonaccountable. These also are less advantageous to the minister because the allowances must be reported as taxable income.

Other Benefits

A number of other benefits may be part of your compensation package as a clergyperson. You should be aware of the benefits and take advantage of them to the extent that you can. One major benefit is employer-sponsored health insurance. If your employer pays your group health insurance policy premiums, this is a tax-free benefit. Health insurance costs can constitute a major part of expenses for most people, and if you are paying the premiums on your own individual health plan in the marketplace, you will likely not see a tax benefit. However, many conference group health plans have a Section 125 provision that allows any portion of the premium paid by the clergyperson to be a pre-tax deduction.

Another major benefit offered to clergy is a pension plan. Pension programs, like the plan administered for United Methodist clergy by Wespath, offer a range of services that can be helpful to you throughout your lifetime. We'll cover some of the retirement planning options in the next clergy chapter, but you should note that your payments into a tax-deferred account can offer you significant benefits over the long term. Your church's contribution to the denominational pension plan are also part of the package provided to you.

Check with your church or denominational staff about other employer-offered benefits such as life insurance and disability insurance for yourself and your family members. If your church provides group life insurance coverage, the first $50,000 of coverage can be tax-free to you.

These insurance options can be critically important in providing for your family in the case of an unexpected illness or accident. Younger clergy (and much of the U.S. population) sometimes neglect this part of their overall financial well-being, and the situations that arise can be tragic and long-lasting. On the other hand, having adequate coverage can make a huge difference in providing a sense of security and well-being.

Moving Expenses

One common benefit provided to clergy is the payment of moving expenses for an incoming pastor. In an itinerant system, such as The United Methodist Church has, moving is a frequent experience for ministers as they are appointed to new ministry settings. The costs associated with moving have usually been paid by the church.

Until 2018, those moving expenses were not reportable to the IRS as income. A change in the tax laws in 2017, however, resulted in the suspension of the provisions in the code that allowed for this tax benefit through the end of 2025. The result of this is that money paid to move clergy by their church must now be reported as income on the minister's Form W-2.

Since moving expenses can easily run to thousands of dollars, clergy who are moving should prepare for the tax implications of their move in their planning. It is not clear whether the suspension will be lifted after December 31, 2025, or what will replace it if it is lifted.

Discussion Questions

- How would you characterize the tax requirements and implications related to clergy salary and benefits?

- What aspects of clergy finances discussed in this section stood out as especially important or helpful to know? Why?

- What have your previous experiences of these requirements and implications been like? How do these past experiences shape your current approach to personal finances?

- Beyond the practical aspects, how do clergypersons' personal finances affect their relationship with God? their relationship with their congregation? What, if anything, is unique about a clergyperson's experience?

- On a scale of one to ten, how would you rate your current understanding and management of how to set up your personal finances with your congregation? Why?

- What obstacles or challenges do you encounter as you work with your congregation to set up your finances each year?
- How could you help your congregation understand the importance of providing insurance as a way of preparing for unknown future events? What biblical passages help us think about the risks of the future? What would your family need if you were to die or not be able to work for several months if disabled?
- What, if anything, will you begin to do differently as a clergyperson as a result of this program?

CHAPTER 3

Giving and Saving

We get lots of messages on how to spend our money, but not so many on the topics covered in this session—giving and saving. Watch enough media and it's easy to believe that the best measure of who we are is what we drive, what we own, or what we look like (enhanced, of course, by the cosmetic and personal hygiene industries). But God introduces different ways to gauge our worth. As creatures who derive our life and being from God, we can't change our value with our purchases. And as stewards of God's gifts, we are called to practices that feel out-of-step with the consumer marketplace.

Giving and saving were the subjects of John Wesley's second and third rules for the use of money. After advising his followers to "gain all you can," which we covered in session 2, Wesley said "save all you can" and "give all you can." These might seem like mixed messages, but for Wesley they worked hand in hand.

Wesley, drawing on the Scriptures and Christian tradition, believed that all things come from God and therefore even our money was a gift. It was, however, a gift to be used and not hoarded or squandered. When he talked about saving, it was not to store up so much treasure that we no longer trust in God. He did believe in wise provision for the necessities of life, but he warned against both excess wealth and frivolous purchases.

Saving for Wesley was a matter of aligning our spending with our values. "Don't throw [your money] away in idle expenses," he warned, "which is just the same as throwing it into the sea."[1] He knew there was a danger in what we might call impulse buying today—it leads to more impulses to buy. "Who would expend anything in gratifying these desires if he considered that to gratify them is to increase them?"[2] he asked.

Similarly, there is a danger in relying on accumulated wealth to give us a sense of self-worth. As Ecclesiastes 5:10 reminds us, "The money lover isn't satisfied with money; neither is the lover of wealth satisfied with income." If neither wasteful spending nor stockpiled wealth can satisfy us, perhaps a more mindful approach that accounts for our relationship with God is called for.

This is where giving helps us remember who we are in God's eyes. If all that we have is a gift, giving becomes a way of expressing gratitude to God. Like the psalmist we might say, "What can I give back to the LORD / for all the good things [God] has done for me?" (Psalm 116:12). It's not only that our giving blesses others and does good in the world, it also helps us reflect the way God works—giving freely as an expression of love.

Wesley outlined clear instructions for giving from his reading of the Bible. After providing for the necessities for ourselves and our household, there should be room to do good to other Christians and to everyone. His guiding question in asking if he should give was, "Am I acting herein, not as a proprietor, but as a steward of my Lord's goods?"[3] If he felt the answer was "yes," he gave. And if he had any doubt, he prayed on that question. When Christians develop the practice of giving, they usually find that their lives open up to experience a more abundant life. Giving may spring from gratitude, but it also seems to grow a more grateful heart. It's not only that we enjoy seeing the good that our giving can do, but that we see more good in the world and in our lives.

Activity: Getting Started

How are you doing with tracking your expenses? What are you finding difficult or helpful in the process?

Giving

Our practices around earning and gaining income reflect our belief about God's intentions for our lives. So, too, does our approach to giving.

Our consumer culture sends us many messages about what it means to give and give well. One of those messages is, "Give if it benefits you." We are responding to this message when the primary motivation for our giving is being recognized for our generosity, or when we give as a tax benefit, or if our giving is to gain influence or notoriety.

At its worst, the message becomes, "Give to get." This attitude can even infect our spiritual life when we believe that our giving is a kind of inducement to God so that God will give us back more. This "prosperity gospel" message has even worked its way into some churches.

Another message we hear is, "Give if there is anything left over." For the vast majority of people, giving comes last in our financial habits. It has been documented that during the most prosperous periods in our recent history, a strange, counterintuitive thing happened—giving actually decreased as a percentage of income. Income increased but spending consumed the additional income. For many, giving is an afterthought rather than a priority.

Yet another message we take in is, "Give out of a sense of duty." Our consumer culture, and sometimes even our churches will guilt us into feeling that we have a duty to give something. The Lord does ask us to give to those who need it, but God is also concerned about why we give, which we'll talk more about below. Giving out of duty or guilt is an empty gesture and different from generous giving, which comes from the heart.

> ## WHAT OUR CONSUMER CULTURE SAYS ABOUT **GIVING**
>
> - Give if it benefits you.
> - Give if there is anything left over.
> - Give out of a sense of duty.
> - Give to get.

> ## **GIVING** AND THE FAITHFUL WAY
>
> - Giving is a response to God's goodness. (James 1:17)
> - God is our source of security. (Matthew 6:19-21; Matthew 6:33)
> - God cares about economic justice. (Luke 4:18)
> - Giving is a way we can bless others and be blessed. (Genesis 12:2-3)

Believing these messages draws us away from the faithful way, and in doing so, it keeps us from experiencing the joy of generosity that God has in mind for us.

The Bible characterizes those who give out of a desire to grow in their discipleship as "generous." A generous giver is one who gives with a joyful attitude and a compassionate heart. Just as a body of water without an outlet becomes stagnant, a life without an outlet for giving becomes a stagnant life. Giving is the channel through which God's love, compassion, and generosity can flow through us.

GENEROUS **GIVER**

One who gives with an obedient will, a joyful attitude, and a compassionate heart.

When we give, we become more of who God designed us to be. Created in God's image, we are made to live in connection and community with others and to share a portion of what we have with others. Simply put, giving changes the lives of not only those who receive, but also those who give.

God calls us to give in response to God's goodness. James 1:17 says, "Every good gift, every perfect gift, comes from above. These gifts come down from the Father, the creator of the heavenly lights, in whose character there is no change at all." Our Creator gives us good things, and so our giving is simply a way to say, "Thank you. I'm so grateful." An important way we show our gratefulness is by making our giving the first obligation of our income. The Old Testament refers to that as "first fruits" giving (Leviticus 23:10 and others).

Second, God is our source of security. In Matthew 6:19-21, Jesus warned his followers not to store up treasures here on earth, where they can be eaten by moths, get rusty, and where thieves break in and steal (or where one economic downturn can wipe them out). Instead, they should store up treasures in heaven. Another way to think of it is not to put your security in wealth, but in the Provider of wealth—not in the gift, but in the Giver.

A third reason God calls us to give is because God cares about economic justice. The growing inequality of resource distribution is one of the great issues facing our world today, and it is creating much conflict in the world. Throughout Scripture, material blessing has been linked to obedience, particularly in reference to justice and compassion for the poor. If God has blessed us beyond what we need, it's so we can help those less fortunate, not just to increase our standard of living. We are called to love. We can give without loving, but we cannot love without giving.

Another reason God wants us to give is to bless others and to be blessed. The relationship between giving and blessing goes all the way back to God's original covenant with Abraham. In Genesis 12:2-3, God tells Abraham that he and his spouse are being blessed in part so that they can be a blessing to others. We miss that joy and blessing in our own lives when we hold on to what we have rather than sharing freely with others.

A final and very important reason for giving is that it breaks the hold money can so easily have on us. Money often equals power, and money can demand our allegiance. When I release money by giving it away, it breaks the hold money can have over me.

Activity: The Generous Giver

After thinking through the faithful way of giving, in what way(s) do you feel God nudging you? Is there an action step God wants you to take?

Even though generous giving is ultimately a matter of the heart, there is a biblical benchmark we can use for giving—the tithe. Historically, the tithe has had three characteristics. Number one, it's a priority—it is the first thing we do with our resources. This is what the Bible calls "first fruits" giving. Second, it has a purpose—to further the work of God in the world. Third, it is a proportion—a tithe is 10 percent of all we receive or earn. In other words, it's proportionate giving. It's God's way of distributing the opportunity to support God's work in the world based upon our ability to do so.

It is important to consider your giving in terms of a percentage of your income, but 10 percent is a goal toward which we can and should move.

> ## PRACTICAL TIPS ON GIVING
>
> - The biblical benchmark for giving is 10 percent of income, which is called a tithe.
> - Begin by giving something.
> - Develop a long-term plan to reach the tithe.
> - Consider your current financial situation and how you can grow in your giving.

For some, financial stresses and losses mean that giving 10 percent is temporarily not feasible. As we gain control of our financial circumstances and grow to be more like our generous God, growing our giving to and even beyond 10 percent becomes easier and more fulfilling. If you are currently giving less than a tithe (10 percent) here are two action steps to prayerfully consider.

First, give something. It may not be very much to begin with, but regardless of your circumstances, start giving. Express your giving as a percentage of your income, and make it your first priority each pay period, making it "first fruits" giving. As you wrestle with how much to give, be careful not to rationalize that you can't give anything. Most of us can think of something we could give up in order to grow in our giving. A lot of people have found that in addition to the joy they receive, there is a new vision and freedom from God that allows the remainder to go further now that they have committed to first fruits giving.

Once you've begun to give a percentage of your income, the second step is to develop a plan to systematically grow your giving toward your goal of 10 percent. As we have said before, goals require plans. Perhaps you commit to increasing your giving by 1 or more percent of your income each year until you are able to give a full tithe.

For some of us, 10 percent is a wonderful goal to aspire to. Give generously, as the Lord leads you, and if you have more to give, don't stop just because you've hit 10 percent. For instance, if you are in a time of life when the mortgage is paid off and you have all the basic possessions you need, at that point you may be able to expand your giving in gratitude to God. You might feel led to give more, and if you can, give more.

Generous giving is ultimately an issue of the heart. The question that flows out of a loving heart is not, "How much of my money should I give to God's work?" Rather, the key question is, "How much of God's money do I need to live on?"

WHAT IS A **TITHE**?

The Hebrew word *ma'aser*, translated as "tithe" throughout the Bible, literally means a "tenth" of something. Traditionally, a tithe is an offering to a church or other faith community that equals 10 percent of your income. The first mention of *ma'aser* occurs in Genesis 14:20, when "Abram gave Melchizedek one-tenth of everything."

> ## MY SPENDING PLAN: GIVING
>
> 1. In your master Spending Plan, enter the amount you are currently giving to your church or other organization as a tithe (this may be 10 percent of your current income, or it may be higher or lower).
> 2. Think back to The Generous Giver activity on page 47. Was there something specific you felt the Lord was asking you to consider about your giving? Based on this, is there an amount you'd like to add in under "Other Contributions"? If so, record that amount as well.

Saving

The Wise Saver

Let's turn now to the third area of our financial lives—Saving. As in the previous areas we've discussed, we want to look beyond the practicality of money and explore the question, "Who are you becoming as a saver? Are you becoming more faithful or more foolish with what has been entrusted to you?"

In the last section, we suggested you begin your Spending Plan by first giving to God. For your next step, we suggest giving to yourself, which is saving. As it relates to saving, the pull of the consumer culture says, "Eat, drink, be merry, and hey, what the heck, charge it!" Embodied in this attitude are two messages the consumer culture sends about saving. The first is, "If you have it, spend it; and if you don't have it, spend it anyway." Our consumer culture not only discourages saving, but encourages spending, even if it puts you in debt.

> ## THE FINAL ACT OF GIVING
>
> On average, 80-90 percent of a person's net worth is in non-liquid assets such as insurance, real estate, or retirement funds. The question is, "How will we be generous and honor God with the final act of giving at our death?" Leaving a legacy of charity and generosity can be a strong testimony to our faith and a wonderful way to support God's work in the world. For help in this area, see "Giving Assets upon One's Death" on page 133 in the Appendix.

The second message is, "It's futile to save. Saving takes too long and you'll never save enough anyway, so why bother?" Many of us have bought into this way of thinking. The savings rate in the United States is one of the lowest of all the developed nations. In fact, in a number of recent years it fell into negative territory. It seems that collectively we actually spent more than we made.

In contrast to the cultural message that saving is futile, the Bible encourages saving, and characterizes those who want to grow in their discipleship by saving as "wise." The wise saver is one who builds, preserves, and invests with discernment. Proverbs 21:20 says, "The wise store up choice food and olive oil, / but fools gulp theirs down" (NIV). In biblical times, food and oil were a form of currency, and notice, the verse doesn't say the rich store up food and oil—it says the wise do so. You don't have to be rich to be a saver.

In this verse, we also see that it's foolish—even sinful—to hoard. We previously discussed the parable of the rich fool with the overflowing barn in Luke 12. Jesus called him a fool for hoarding his excess. Both of these Scriptures teach that it is wise to save for the unexpected but it's foolish to stockpile beyond our needs. So, if it's wise to save but foolish and sinful to hoard, how can we tell when saving has crossed the line into hoarding?

One way to guard against this tendency is to see saving as putting money aside for appropriate goals, such as retirement and college education. There are a lot of appropriate savings goals out there, and those goals may be different for different people. But the key is that all along the way we're prayerfully reflecting on those goals and not stockpiling beyond our needs, using our goals as excuses to build bigger barns.

As we begin a discipline of saving, it's helpful to understand our tendencies and what shaped our financial behavior early on. For example, some of us may

WHAT OUR CONSUMER CULTURE SAYS ABOUT **SAVING**

- If you have it, spend it, and if you don't have it, spend it anyway.
- It is futile to save.

WISE **SAVER**

One who builds, preserves, and invests with discernment.

have discovered in the pre-work, on the Money Motivation Quiz, that money represents love and personal relationships. We are more relationally oriented and tend to spend money on others rather than preparing for our own futures. We may need to be more disciplined in our saving habits. For others, money represents security. If so, some of us may have the inclination to keep more of it than we reasonably need just to be safe and secure. Another way of getting helpful personal insights is by reviewing the Money Autobiography in the pre-work. Many of our behaviors surrounding money are governed by events that happened to us early in life, but we don't even know it. When those influences are revealed, we can make decisions about whether to continue those behaviors or not.

Another way to avoid the "bigger barns" syndrome is to answer the difficult but critical question, "When is enough, enough?" This is not an easy question to answer, but it is key to getting to the heart of the issue. The problem for many of us in deciding what is enough is that we can always come up with another "What if?" scenario that allows us to say, "Well, I just have to save a little more in case that happens!" But in this kind of thinking, you soon realize that enough will never be enough.

> ## SAVING AND THE FAITHFUL WAY
>
> - It is wise to save. (Proverbs 21:20)
> - It is foolish, even sinful, to hoard. (Luke 12:16-21)
> - Saving is putting money aside for appropriate goals.
> - Hoarding is stockpiling beyond our needs or using our goals as excuses to build "bigger barns."
> - How can we avoid the "bigger barns" syndrome? By understanding our tendencies and realizing when enough is enough. (Ecclesiastes 5:10 NLT)

Activity: Your Money Tendency

Because it's important to be aware of our money tendencies and how they impact us, let's take some time to consider them. Following, are four main motivations that most of us have when it comes to money.

1. Check the box on the following page that you feel applies to you when it comes to money. If you completed the Money Motivation Quiz in the pre-work, refer to the results of that quiz.

Money is important to me because it gives me:

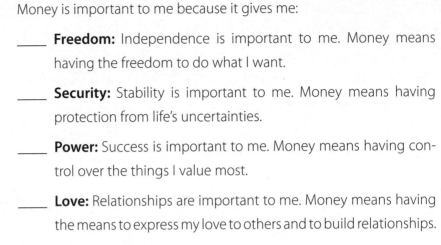

_____ **Freedom:** Independence is important to me. Money means having the freedom to do what I want.

_____ **Security:** Stability is important to me. Money means having protection from life's uncertainties.

_____ **Power:** Success is important to me. Money means having control over the things I value most.

_____ **Love:** Relationships are important to me. Money means having the means to express my love to others and to build relationships.

2. What is one way your money tendency impacts you?

3. What is one step you can take to begin limiting that impact?

4. What did you learn from your Money Autobiography pre-work? How do you think your past experience with money shapes your present situation or attitude?

The Benefits of Saving

Saving is a biblical trait worth embracing, but how does saving work in a practical sense? Saving is money you keep. When you buy a $65 sweater on sale for $40, you do not "save" $25—you spend $40. The next time you see a sale ad that says, "Buy now and save 50 percent!" see that ad for what it's really saying—"Buy now and spend 50 percent!" Saving in this situation would mean not buying the item and instead saving 100 percent of that money.

Saving is not money we have somehow lost or given up the use of. Saving is actually spending, but it's future spending. We save money now to have it available at a future time. A huge benefit of saving is that it allows the very powerful force of compounding to work in our favor. When placed in an account that uses compound interest, that money grows exponentially.

For example: let's assume we invested $100. For the sake of simplicity, let's say we are able to earn 10 percent annual interest on that money. At 10 percent interest, the $100 would earn $10 in interest, and we'd have $110 at the end of one year. If we then left the entire $110 invested for a second year, we'd earn $11 in interest. The additional dollar earned the second year is compound interest, the interest earned on interest.

Compounding is an incredibly powerful concept. We can see the impact of compound interest in the graphs below. These graphs show the growth that occurs by compound interest if we save $100 per month at 10 percent over a twenty-year period and a forty-year period.

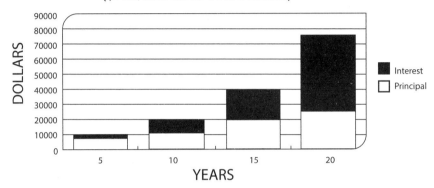

The Power of Compound Interest over 20 Years
($100/month at 10% interest)

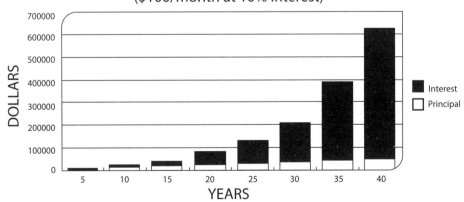

The Power of Compound Interest over 40 Years
($100/month at 10% interest)

The figure of 10 percent is used here for ease of mathematical illustration. A more realistic return for your investments might be 6.5 percent or 7 percent.

By year twenty, the last bar on the right-hand side of the first graph, we will have put in $24,000 ($1,200 per year for twenty years). That's represented by the bottom portion of the bar. The entire bar represents the total amount of money we now have: over $76,500. The difference between the two, represented by the top portion of the bar, is what we have gained through compound interest. And if we were to extend this graph out to forty years, you would have put in $48,000 and have almost $637,000.

One of the things you can see about compounding from those graphs is that it begins slowly but then grows at an increasing rate. The fruit of the Spirit required to be a good saver is patience. Time is your greatest ally, and there is no better time than right now to start saving and having compound interest work for you—24 hours a day, 7 days a week, 365 days a year. You work for your money, so let your money work for you through compounding interest.

Remember that the power of compounding interest can work against you as well. Compound interest is the reason that credit card bills can swell so dramatically. By eliminating debt and faithfully contributing to your savings, you can make sure compound interest works in your best interest.

Another financial concept worth mentioning is what is called the "opportunity cost" of money. We once heard a man explain it this way: He pointed to the nice sweater he was wearing and asked the group how much they thought it cost him. People would state a dollar amount, such as $50 or $70, and he replied that they were guessing at what he paid for it, not what it cost him. He went on to explain that he paid $65 for the sweater, but it actually cost him much more than that. Why? Because if, at thirty years old, he had not spent that $65 and had instead invested it in a stock fund that returned 10 percent until he was 65 years old, the

> ## COMPOUNDING APPLIES TO BOTH SIDES OF THE FINANCIAL EQUATION: SAVING AND SPENDING.
>
> There's a cumulative effect of a little savings over time, and there's a cumulative effect of a little bit of overspending over time (that is, debt). An in-depth explanation of the principle of the cumulative effect and some interesting examples of the impact of compound interest appear on page 135 in the Appendix, "The Cumulative Effect of Little Things over an Extended Period."

$65 would have doubled in value every seven years—or five times until he was 65. That works out to be $2,080, which made the sweater he was wearing quite expensive!

It's something to consider, right? Obviously we have to make purchases all the time throughout our lives, but it's sobering to realize that we can spend money on anything, but we can only spend it once!

As we talked about earlier this session, when we come to our income, or what we have received, giving back to God should be our first priority and saving should be our second. We understand that, for many of us who haven't been in the habit of saving anything, this can seem daunting; but the key thing to remember is that we can all save something. Right now for you that might not be a whole lot, but it can be something, and it's important to start now.

Three Categories of Savings

Savings fall into three categories and should be prioritized in the following order: emergency savings, replacement savings, and long-term savings.

Emergency Savings

Emergency savings prepare you for the unexpected, such as sudden unemployment or a serious illness. These emergency reserves prevent you from having to incur credit card debt when the unexpected happens. A generally accepted goal for emergency savings is a minimum of three months' worth of basic living expenses, such as housing, food, and transportation costs. If you can't do that yet, a good starting goal is to save $500 or $1,000 as soon as possible and grow from there. One family worked toward that goal by having a garage sale of all the things they knew in their hearts they didn't need and put that money into savings. The key is to start saving something.

Since you need to be able to get these funds quickly when an emergency strikes, they should be kept in accounts you have easy access to, such as a money market fund or a bank or credit union savings account.

Replacement Savings

Replacement savings are for large expected purchases, things we know will need to be replaced someday such as refrigerators and cars, and for major home repairs like a new roof or heating and cooling system. (For a list of the expected life spans and replacement cost of common household items, see pages 137–138 of the Appendix.) Since these needs are more predictable, replacement savings could be invested in short-term CD's that come due before the predicted time for the replacement.

Sometimes in the early stages of building replacement funds, the line can be blurred between emergency and replacement savings. For example, if the water heater goes out, is that an emergency or a replacement? Since we might anticipate that at some point the water heater would need to be replaced, it's really a replacement cost. But until we have replacement savings built up, if we have to replace something that's a necessity (like the water heater) and don't have replacement savings for it, it becomes an emergency and we use our emergency savings. However, we should be very careful how we determine what is an "emergency."

An excellent approach to ensure that you actually save money for emergencies and replacement savings is to have a small amount direct deposited into your designated account every paycheck, if your employer allows for that option. And, as we discussed in session 2, you could also set aside a portion of your next raise to build up these funds as well.

> **DON'T BORROW FROM YOUR RETIREMENT FUNDS, SUCH AS IRAS OR 401KS.**
>
> This is seldom a good idea. For an explanation of why borrowing from retirement funds is not wise, see the information on pages 138–139 of the Appendix.

Long-Term Savings

Long-term savings are for planned circumstances that are down the road, such as retirement or a child's college education. A great tip for long-term savings is to take advantage of your employer's retirement plan, if that is available to you, and definitely participate if there are matching funds provided. That's free money!

MY SPENDING PLAN: SAVING

Let's take time now to fill in the savings category on your Spending Plan.

1.   Start by calculating the amount of emergency savings you might need. Consider a minimum of three months' worth of basic living expenses such as housing, food, and transportation. Write that amount here:

2.   Consider your current financial situation. What amount are you currently putting toward savings every month? Write that amount here:

3.   Based on your answers to the above, do you need to increase what you are saving for emergencies? If so, what amount would you like to contribute to your emergency savings every month?

     Can you make this amount your goal for the next few months? Add this amount into your Spending Plan.

4.   If you already have an emergency savings fund, consider your goals for replacement or long-term savings. Is there an amount you can add to these funds every month? Add those amounts into your Spending Plan.

5.   Fill in the savings category on your Spending Plan form.

You now have a goal for savings. Good job!

Activity: Wrapping Up

1.   Were there any new insights for you about giving and if so, what impact might they have?

2. What aspect of saving is most difficult for you and what action steps might you take to make savings easier?

3. Continue to record your expenses this week.

CHAPTER 4

Understanding and Eliminating Debt

Nothing worries homeowners like a water stain appearing in a place they didn't expect it. A suspicious spot in a ceiling or floorboard is a sign that an unseen leak is attacking the integrity of the house and likely has been for a while. It usually means that a major repair to the roof or the plumbing is on the horizon. And if the stain is left to spread, the situation only grows worse, despite our best efforts to ignore it.

Debt can work the same sort of worry in our lives. It appears each month on our credit card statement and, if unaddressed, has a tendency to grow. It's possible to ignore it, often for a long time. Credit card issuers make it seem easy to manage the debt with minimum monthly payments that don't hint at the true cost of what we owe or how long it will take to repay. But the worry creeps in and keeps us from feeling the kind of financial well-being we would like to feel.

The worries caused by debt hint at a deeper disturbance in our soul. In a sermon on Jesus's teaching in the Sermon on the Mount that we should not have cares about the future, John Wesley compares Jesus's attitude with the worries we feel when the future seems threatened. Jesus, Wesley says, "forbids only that care which poisons the blessings of to-day, by fear of what may be to-morrow; which cannot enjoy the present plenty, through apprehensions of future want."[1]

Debt is one of those things that makes us apprehensive about the future and keeps us from flourishing as God intends. Wesley also believed that anyone who had enough to eat and clothes to wear could be considered rich. But when debt enters the picture, even when "a person may have more than necessaries and conveniences . . . [that person] is not a rich man, how much money soever he has in his hands."[2]

Wesley drew on a particular verse in Paul's letter to the Romans to frame his understanding of debt. Romans 13:8 advises, "Don't be in debt to anyone, except for the obligation to love each other. Whoever loves another person has fulfilled the Law." He understood that debt not only creates worries within us, it also harms our ability to show love to one another. When we are hampered by debt, we don't have the freedom to live out the simple rules of earning, saving, and giving we have explored in earlier sessions.

Understanding the corrosive effects of debt requires us to consider the ways our impulses in the present impact our relationship with the future. In this consumer culture in which so many projects are built on the creative use of debt and in which we are encouraged to take on debt ourselves, recovering a healthy sense of the cost of incurring debt is both countercultural and spiritual. We grow in our discipleship as we look at the future with a clear and humble understanding of the resources we have been given and a trust that God will provide for us a peace no credit card could ever manage to give.

This is not to say that we will be able to avoid debt entirely. Most of us will face situations in our lives when we will have to take on a major expense and incur some debt in the process. In this session we will explore when it may be appropriate to do that and how to be wise as we do. We'll also talk about those areas where we might be tempted to spend beyond our means in ways that have long-term implications for our financial health.

For many of us, this area of our financial lives is the hardest to confront. Debt is tied up with so many feelings, from anxiety and worry to shame. But having confidence that we can face our debt worries with a plan can free us for different kinds of feelings, such as gratitude, generosity, and an openness to the future. This is the kind of life God calls us to live as we discover what it's like to trust God.

Activity: Getting Started

What are you discovering as a result of tracking your expenses? [Do you see any patterns or areas of your spending that seem to need attention?]

The fourth area of our financial lives that we will explore is debt. As in each of the other areas, debt is about more than just finances; so we continue to ask the questions, Who are you as a debtor? Are you becoming more faithful or more foolish in relation to your debt?

Statistics indicate that, in many ways, we as a country are becoming more foolish as it relates to this area of our financial lives. But before we review the negative aspects of most debt, we can acknowledge that there is such a thing as "OK" debt. OK debt has two characteristics: First, it's used for something that has the strong potential to increase in value, so it has an economic justification, because the cost to borrow is less than the economic value or gain received. An example would be to take out a reasonable first mortgage on a home that should increase in value over time.

That means that debt on a depreciating or consumptive item—meaning an item you use up—is never OK debt. Debt on that new car that's worth thousands of dollars less the moment you drive it off the lot is not OK debt. However, many people have car loans and later on we'll see a very reasonable way those can be avoided over time.

The second characteristic of OK debt is that it will be able to be repaid under today's circumstances, not some hoped-for circumstances in the future. That means it's okay to have the money in your current budget to pay your monthly mortgage payment, but it's not okay to incur debt today on that sixty-inch flat screen because you're sure you'll get the bonus or commission next month to pay it off.

That being said, let's take a look at the pull of the consumer culture when it comes to debt, and then explore debt with the faithful way in mind.

IS **DEBT** EVER OK?

"OK" debt has two characteristics:

1. It is incurred on something that has the strong potential to increase in value, such as a home (not a depreciating or consumptive item, such as clothing or electronics).

2. It can be repaid under today's circumstances—not hoped-for circumstances in the future.

CAUTIOUS DEBTOR

One who avoids entering into debt, is careful and strategic when incurring debt, and always repays debt.

The Cautious Debtor

In our consumer culture today, one widely believed myth is that debt is expected and unavoidable. Unfortunately, a lot of people have bought into this myth and the consequences are staggering. According to a 2020 report, based upon the amount of credit card debt and the average interest on that debt (which happens to be 16.6 percent), well over $121 billion was paid in 2019 in credit card interest.[3] (That doesn't include mortgage interest.) That explains why credit card companies try so very hard to enlist us as their customers, and their efforts are very seductive and often successful.

WHAT OUR CONSUMER CULTURE SAYS ABOUT DEBT

Debt is expected and unavoidable.

In some cases, we incur debt for reasons beyond our control, such as a health crisis, the loss of a job, or an accident. Those are difficult situations, and it is important to let your creditors know of your circumstances in those cases to see if you can get some relief on your payments. But if most of us who are in consumer debt are honest, we would acknowledge that our debt could have been avoided if we had resisted the temptation of immediate gratification and lived within our means.

Today it is increasingly easier to get into debt. Historically, in order to borrow money, you had to provide evidence that you had the means to repay it. Now, with over three billion credit card solicitations occurring annually, that is obviously no longer true. It's really very easy to get into debt and stay there. Rumor has it that some credit card companies intentionally target people who have recently declared bankruptcy since by law they can't file bankruptcy again for seven years. And the interest rates charged are often in the high 20 percent range.

The Economic Danger of Debt

The implication of normalizing debt is the belief that there are really no negative consequences to debt. In reality, there are serious economic and spiritual dangers to debt. The economic danger is that compound interest works against you.

Take a close look at the graphic on the next page, which shows the power of compound interest on your debt. In this graphic, you can see how $100 borrowed at 20 percent grows into a much larger debt over time. At 20 percent interest, compounding will double the amount owed in a little less than three and a half years. This shows how the burden of debt can bury you quicker than you can imagine. In fact, credit card companies now have the right to change your interest rate for any reason—this is called "universal default." If you're late on any of your credit cards, or even something like a utility bill, all of your credit card companies have the right to raise your interest to an alarmingly high rate.

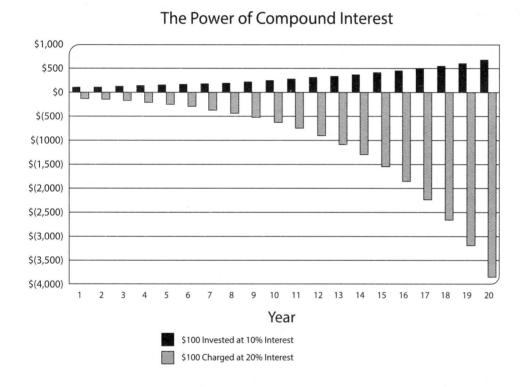

The Power of Compound Interest

■ $100 Invested at 10% Interest
□ $100 Charged at 20% Interest

The Spiritual Danger of Debt

That's all very sobering and it drives home the fact that we don't want to let ourselves get into that situation, and neither does God. The Bible warns us to be cautious about debt, which makes sense with what we've already stated. The cautious debtor is one who seeks to avoid entering into debt, is careful and strategic when incurring debt, and always repays debt.

There are spiritual dangers of debt. One of them is that debt presumes on the future. Every time we take on debt, we are presuming that we will be able to pay it back. Credit advertising says, "You can afford a $220 monthly payment," and while that may be true this month and next, it may not be true for the life of the loan. James 4:14 warns, "You don't really know about tomorrow. What is your life? You are a mist that appears for only a short while before it vanishes." So be sure that any debt you take on can be repaid under current circumstances, not some circumstances you think will come about in the future.

Another spiritual danger is that, in taking on debt, we may erode our trust in God, that God will be able to reveal to us new dimensions of love and provision within our current means. For example, let's say there's something you really wanted but don't have the money for. You know it may not be the wise thing to do, but you really want it so you go out and get it with your credit card. What if your patience and forbearance helped you to see how the thing you wanted might be available in another way or at a lower cost? Maybe the item was available used. Maybe you might receive it as a gift. Or maybe, in waiting you determine that you really didn't need it at all.

DEBT AND THE FAITHFUL WAY

- Repay debt.
- Avoid debt.
- Debt presumes on the future and erodes our trust in God to show love and provision to us.
- Discipline and contentment are better values than immediate gratification.
- Envy and greed can drive us into debt.

Speaking to his disciples, Jesus said that, in terms of worrying about providing for our daily needs, "All the nations of the world long for these things. Your Father knows that you need them. Instead, desire his kingdom and these things will be given to you as well" (Luke 12:30-31).

The third spiritual danger is that debt is often fostered by our envy and greed. We all have a natural inclination to want more, and debt and credit can be used to encourage that envious, greedy part of us. "Then Jesus said to them, 'Watch out! Guard yourself against all kinds of greed. After all, one's life isn't determined by one's possessions, even when someone is very wealthy'" (Luke 12:15).

Finally, there is a spiritual danger to the society because of debt. In the Bible there are many warnings about lending money at interest because of the potential for lenders to abuse the debtor, increasing the burden, especially on the poor. In the instructions for the Israelite community, Moses gives the warning, "You shall not charge interest on loans to another Israelite, interest on money, interest on provisions, interest on anything that is lent" (Deuteronomy 23:19, NRSV). The predatory practices of paycheck lenders in our own day reveal how pervasive this danger is.

It's clear that in the area of debt, the "wisdom" of the consumer culture can pull us away from the faithful way. Don't be discouraged. This study can begin to free you from the burdens that debt may have placed on you.

Breaking Down Debt

It is helpful to understand that there are primarily six kinds of debt:

1. Home mortgage
2. Auto
3. Education
4. Business
5. Consumer (credit cards)
6. Medical

In this chapter, we focus on credit card debt, which we often refer to as consumer debt. We're going to focus on this type of debt, because, no question about it, it's the easiest debt to get into and the one that gets us into the most trouble.

Let's be clear, it's not practical to not ever use credit cards, but you must do so wisely. For example, when you travel, you need a card to hold a hotel reservation or car rental. It's more secure to purchase things online with a credit card. It's convenient and a secure form of payment. Sometimes you get low interest rates and even cash back or frequent flier miles to boot. Yes, there can be some advantages.

But the fact is that credit cards, and debit cards too, can encourage us to violate almost every principle of good personal money management.

There appear to be two explanations for the phenomenon of spending more when using a credit card. First of all, using a credit card is psychologically different than using cash. Let's say you make a purchase amounting to $37.88. The cashier takes your credit card and puts a receipt in front of you. You sign it and walk out the door. From a psychological standpoint, that transaction is very different than if you give the cashier a twenty-dollar bill, a ten, a five, and three singles, and are left with only twelve cents in your hand. All you did in the first transaction was sign your name on a piece of paper. But in the cash transaction, you received very tangible evidence that the money was no longer available to you. You saw those bills go to someone else and know that you just have twelve cents left. Even making a purchase and subtracting the amount in your records allows you to see your new balance, so there will be some awareness that you now have less than you did before. There's just no such feedback when all we do is sign a piece of paper.

The other explanation for why we tend to spend more when we use a credit card is that, unless you download or monitor your transactions regularly, you have no awareness of total charges until the end of the billing period. Have you ever logged into your account or opened your statement and been surprised at the balance you saw on your accounts? Maybe you even thought, *The bank must have made a mistake*, but when you started looking at all the purchases, you realized that you were indeed the one who made all those purchases. If most of us had to guess what we've charged on our credit or debit cards since the last billing statement, we'd almost always guess a lower amount.

In the world we live in, virtually all of us have need for a credit card. But it might be interesting to experiment for a month in using the card as little as possible and see what difference that might make, psychologically and monetarily.

Rules for Using Credit Cards

Since we're all using cards these days, here are three rules to live by, especially if you're already fighting credit card debt:

1. Use credit cards only for budgeted items.

   For some budgeted items, a credit card is especially safe to use. For example, buying gas. You're unlikely to get carried away and overfill the tank and let it run all over the ground just because you're using your credit card. But, in many other cases, you will need to ask the question, "Is this in the Spending Plan?"

2. Pay the balance in full every month.

   Remember, if you've used the card only for budgeted items, the money will be there to pay the balance due. Doing this will avoid all interest charges.

3. Choose the best card for your needs.

   If you opt to use a credit card, research your options and find a card with an introductory bonus or reward system (like cash back or frequent flier miles) that increases its value.

Tips for Using Credit and Debit Cards

Some additional tips to keep in mind: First, have only one card that you use regularly—with perhaps just one other card as backup. That can reduce the temptation to overspend and will simplify bill paying. Select a card with no annual fee and then shred all other offers for additional cards.

Second, consider the wise use of a debit card. Ideally, a debit card provides you with the convenience of a credit card, but instead of adding to your debt, reaches directly into your account for the funds spent. Using a debit card is like writing a check that clears instantly. This, of course, means the money actually has to be there before it's spent. Just be aware that the transaction hits your account immediately, so in theory you could not overspend. No money in account, no transaction. But the problem is that many banks allow the transaction to go through and then impose a non-sufficient fund fee that can be more than $40, or allow an "overdraft protection" on your account that carries a fee and high interest rate. So be very sure you understand how your individual account works.

If you use a debit card write down each transaction and subtract it from your balance in your check ledger, app, or online account as you go to make sure you don't overdraw. In fact, it's a good idea to record all your transactions, whether using a credit or debit card. Recording the transaction provides concrete evidence that you now have less money for other things and allows you to reconcile your total with what the bank says online.

One other note we want to mention. Many of us make online purchases. In this scenario, the psychological factors at work are all on the side of you spending more when you buy online. Remember, every purchase, including online purchases, needs to be part of your Spending Plan. And again, record those online purchases right away on paper, online, or in a budgeting app.

Activity: Your Credit Cards

In the space below, write down one action step you want to take regarding your credit or debit card(s). Maybe you need to commit to recording your purchases or limit yourself to only using your cards for budgeted items. What is one step you can implement today?

> Action Step:

Paying Down Debt

For those of us who do have credit card debt, let's take a look at some examples of how one credit card can be paid down over time and the impact of only paying the minimum payment.

You owe $7,200 @ 18%		
Minimum Payment = 3% of the balance or $10—whichever is greater		
You Pay	**Total Paid**	**Time**
$ Minimum/month	$14,277	20 yrs. 11 mos.
$216/month	$10,150	47 mos.
$216+100/month	$8,848	28 mos.

The example (above) assumes you have a credit card balance of $7,200 with 18 percent interest and a minimum payment per month of 3 percent of the balance. (In many cases the minimum payment is less than 3 percent, which would make the example even more dramatic.)

Let's further assume you follow the credit card company's plan and pay only the minimum payment each month. The first month you pay 3 percent of $7,200, or $216. Over time, as you make some progress on reducing the $7,200, the minimum payment also decreases and you pay a little less each month. Following that plan, your repayment will add up to almost $14,300 and take twenty years and eleven months to pay off. Of course, this assumes that you don't use the credit card to make any new charges during this time.

But suppose you pay $216 a month until the loan is completely repaid. That is, you don't decrease your payments when the credit card company says you can. It might take some discipline to pay more than you have to, but your total repayment drops from over $14,000 to $10,150 and the debt gets paid off in a little under four years. That's a savings of $4,000 and seventeen years faster.

Let's consider an even better possibility. Suppose you were able to pay an extra $100 per month on top of the $216. The total repayment drops to $8,848 and is repaid in only twenty-eight months!

There are two important comparisons in these illustrations. First is the $8,848 repayment versus over $14,000. That's a big reduction. The second and even more important comparison is getting out of debt in just over two years instead of sweating it out for almost twenty-one years! We can guess what is going through a lot of your minds: *"Great in theory, but where am I going to get an extra $100 a month?"* That's a very valid

KEY QUESTION

Are you committed enough to freeing yourself from debt to find a little over three dollars a day somewhere in your expenditures that could go to debt repayment?

PROCESS FOR ACCELERATING DEBT REPAYMENT

1. Incur no new debt!
2. List all your debts in order from smallest to largest.
3. Pay off your smallest debt first.
4. As a debt is repaid, add the amount you were paying to the next largest debt.
5. Continue that strategy until all debts are paid.

For more guidance on creating a debt repayment plan, see "Establishing a Debt Repayment Plan" on page 141 in the Appendix.

question when you're already in debt and struggling, but here's a question to consider, "Are you committed enough to freeing yourself from the bondage of debt to find a little over three dollars a day somewhere in your expenditures to go to debt repayment? A little over $3 a day adds up to the $100 a month we're looking for.

Accelerating Debt Repayment

Assuming we find some ways to come up with some extra money, let's look at an actual process for accelerating debt repayment.

First, and most important, incur no new debt. You have to take a stand that you will live strictly according to your Spending Plan. That's fundamental. Even though there are wise ways to use credit cards, if you're carrying balances on your cards, it is better to use them as little as possible until the balances are paid off. Hopefully you're in the process of saving up an emergency fund that will cover any unexpected costs, which will eliminate the need to use your cards for that purpose.

Second, list all your debts. It's not fun, but it's necessary, and if you've done your pre-work, you already have the list (see "What I Owe/What I Own" worksheet). Then arrange the list from smallest to largest debt. We're going to pay off your smallest debt first. The strategy is to take the smallest debt and, in addition to its minimum payment, pay whatever additional money you've been able to come up with toward that monthly payment. You could argue that the greatest savings would occur by attacking the debt with the highest interest rate first. While this is true, the psychological benefit of starting with the smallest debts and getting one or more paid off quickly far exceeds the couple extra bucks it may cost in interest.

Third, as a debt is repaid, add the amount you were paying to the next largest debt, adding it to that debt's minimum monthly payment. Do not decrease your total monthly debt repayment until all debts are completely paid off. This creates a cumulative effect of adding the payment for the last debt to the next one and provides tremendous momentum to accelerate your debt repayment.

Let's take a look at the Sample Debt Reduction Plan that appears on the next page.

SAMPLE DEBT REDUCTION PLAN

Item	Amount Owed	Interest	Minimum Monthly Payment	Additional Payment $ 150	Payment Plan and Pay-off Dates				
					3 Months	6 Months	15 Months	22 Months	26 Months
Target	$372	18.0	$15	$165	paid!				
Doctor	$550	0	$20	$20	$185	paid!			
Visa	$980	19.0	$40	$40	$40	$225	paid!		
MasterCard	$2369	16.9	$50	$50	$50	$50	$275	paid!	
Auto	$7200	6.9	$259	$259	$259	$259	$259	$534	paid!
Total	$12,471		$384	$534	$534	$534	$534	$534	0

- The first and second columns list to whom the debt is owed and the amount owed. Debts are listed in the order of lowest to highest amount.
- The third and fourth columns list the interest rate and the minimum monthly payment for each debt.
- The fifth column indicates the amount of additional payment above the minimum that can be made and adds that amount to the minimum payment for the first (smallest) debt listed.
- The remaining columns show how, as each debt is paid, the payment for it is rolled down to the next debt. Pay-off dates can be calculated in advance or simply recorded as they are achieved.

_____

You'll notice this person has arranged her or his debts in order, lowest to highest, and written down the minimum payments required by each. This person also determined he or she could pay $150 in addition to the minimum payments. The $150 was then added to the $15 minimum payment of the smallest debt and that enabled it to be paid off in just three months. Then the total of $165, which the person was paying on that debt was added to the $20 minimum payment of the next largest debt and it was paid off in three more months. That process was continued until the entire original debt of $12,471 was paid off in twenty-six months!

It is vital that you incur no new debt in this process. It will take discipline to do it, but you won't make progress if you are continuing to incur new debt as the old is being paid. However, if you stop going further into debt and take the first small step toward repayment, you will have completely reversed the direction you were heading. And when you've paid off each of your debts, celebrate with those who have helped you in the process and give thanks to God.

> You can find a blank Debt Reduction Plan in your Appendix on page 163, and an electronic version of the plan can be found at abingdonpress.com/savinggrace.

MY SPENDING PLAN: DEBT

1. Using your pre-work information from the "What I Owe/What I Own" worksheet, list each of your debts and fill in the monthly minimum payments on your Spending Plan form. (If you did not complete the pre-work, estimate your monthly minimum payment for each debt.)
2. Set a tentative goal for how much additional payment you plan to make each month.
3. Apply this additional payment to your smallest debt on your Spending Plan.

The Benefits of Debt Repayment

Now that you've entered an amount for your debt payments on your Spending Plan, consider this additional motivation for you to make debt repayment a top priority. You may not have looked at it this way, but debt repayment is a great investment. You may be looking for a good investment, maybe one that will spin off big returns so you can pay off your debt, but what we want to stress is that you already have a great investment opportunity. Every dollar you use to pay off debt results in an immediate, tax-free, guaranteed investment, with a high rate of return because you're getting out from under those high interest payments.

For many of us, debt is often the symptom, not the problem. You may be recovering from a crisis or job loss, or for many it could be a result of lifelong over-spending patterns you grew up with in your family of origin. Perhaps it is connected to feelings of insecurity or a lack of self-esteem. Take whatever steps are necessary to discover and eliminate the root issue behind your debt. Solicit the help of a trusted friend(s) who will support you in this endeavor, or perhaps enlist the help of a counselor. It is worth your time and effort to rid yourself of behaviors that feed the problem. Avoid window-shopping and unsubscribe your email from retailers that constantly tout their online offers. There's a term in behavioral psychology called the "law of exposure." It says that the things we are exposed to are the things we think about, which then become the things we act upon. Marketers understand this and promote a process in which a product "evolves" from being a luxury, to a convenience, to a necessity. So take some time to think about your spending temptations and how to limit your exposure to them.

The pull of the consumer culture is so very strong in this area. Pray for God to guide and encourage you to take the right steps and make the difficult choices necessary to move out of consumer debt and into financial well-being and faithfulness.

> ## DEBT **REPAYMENT** IS A GREAT INVESTMENT!
>
> - Immediate
> - Tax Free
> - Guaranteed
> - High rate of return

> ## **DEBT** IS OFTEN THE **SYMPTOM**, NOT THE PROBLEM
>
> - Discover and eliminate the root of the issue.
> - Limit your exposure to temptation.
> - Give up on one-upping your neighbors.

Activity: Wrapping Up

1. What new insights about consumer debt did you get from this session?

2. Do you agree that spending with a credit card is psychologically different than using cash? Are there examples from your own experience?

3. Look at the amount of money now going to your debt repayment. Imagine the well-being you will feel when you are out from under that burden and the financial goals you can achieve with those resources. If you want to, use the space below to write down your thoughts and reflections about how being debt-free could affect your life.

4. This week try not to use your credit card and note how that feels.

5. Use the records you've been keeping to review the items in the Household/Personal category of your "What I Spend" worksheet from your pre-work. We will talk more in the next session about how to reduce these expenses, but do any areas stand out to you as perhaps being too high?

Planning Ahead—Retirement

The biblical story of Ruth is not often thought of as tale of retirement. After all, Ruth herself is a younger woman whose story seems to be about mere survival. But what makes Ruth an extraordinary character is the way her resourcefulness becomes a blessing for all those around her, including her mother-in-law, Naomi, who, through much of the story, faces her older years with little to no security.

When Naomi's husband dies in Moab, a foreign land, Naomi returns home to Bethlehem trailed by Ruth, whose own husband, Naomi's son, has also died. In Bethlehem, Ruth, despite being a foreigner, takes advantage of the gleaning traditions of Israel that allowed the vulnerable members of the community to pick up the grain left behind as the barley harvest was reaped.

She catches the eye of the field owner, Boaz, who is a near kinsman to Naomi. In some eyebrow-raising encounters with Boaz, Ruth challenges him to follow up on his responsibilities to his larger family, another source of social security in that time period. While the book often gets reduced to a simple love story between the two or a tale of Ruth's loyalty to Naomi, it can also be read as a story of Ruth's resourcefulness. To be sure, as a woman in the ancient Near East, Ruth's options would have been limited by the largely patriarchal culture she inhabited. Yet her resourcefulness stands out nevertheless. This sharp and clever woman uses every avenue available to seek God's blessings for herself and her family.

CLERGY VIDEOS

Videos for the clergy sessions are available at AmplifyMedia.com (search Saving Grace) and are included on the *Saving Grace* DVD.

Every clergyperson preparing for retirement would do well to follow the model of Ruth. There are many considerations for clergy and many potential avenues to explore for developing assets that will sustain you in retirement. The earlier in your career that you begin preparing, the easier that process will be. But even for clergy who are nearing the end of their ministerial career, there are significant decisions to make that can help make your retirement better.

In this chapter we are going to explore some of the aspects of retirement that are of particular interest to clergy. We will cover housing, pensions, insurance, wills, and estate planning. You will find that in some of these areas there are many resources to help, especially if you are part of a denominational pension plan. There are also important options to choose from that can have short- and long-term implications for your retirement. You will need the trust and confidence of Ruth to navigate these decisions and make the choices that are right for you and your family.

Planning for Retirement

One key question to answer is: *When does my retirement begin?* As the economy changes and people are living and working longer, retiring at 65 is not a given, with many working beyond that age. Alternatively, family or health concerns may dictate an earlier retirement age. What is the age you have set for your retirement goal? Recognizing that life changes may impact that planned retirement date, having a goal in mind is important for your planning.

A second question is: *How much money will I need in retirement?* This question also has variables that impact your answer. If you would like to have resources in your retirement that give you 80 percent of your current income, that is one aspect of your planning. You also need to estimate how long you will need that income. While none of us knows the length of our lives, you want to prepare for the full post-retirement period of your life. Let's pray for long life!

Having conversations with a financial planner early in your career can help you chart a course toward the answers to these questions. But you also shouldn't ignore one simple fact that is found throughout this book: the earlier you plan and save, the better your prospects for having a sufficient amount for retirement.

Through compounding interest, a small investment left in place for a long period of time can reap huge returns. This is why an early commitment to savings can make such a huge difference to your retirement.

One way to begin is to put as much money as you can into 403(b) tax-sheltered annuity plans, such as those offered by many churches and denominational groups. Contributions to these plans are tax-deferred, meaning that you do not have to pay income taxes on them until you begin to withdraw them in retirement. They are also not subject to Social Security taxes, even when the benefits are received.

You can also explore other avenues for investment that have tax advantages. You can contribute up to the maximum annual amount into a nondeductible Roth Individual Retirement Account (IRA), which offers tax-free growth and tax-free withdrawals in retirement as long as you have owned the account for five years and are age 59 1/2 or older when you begin withdrawals (the basis in a Roth IRA may be withdrawn without penalty at any time). You can also do the same for a regular deductible IRA, in which your taxes on the earnings are deferred.

In addition, as you are able, you should explore other types of investments such as stocks and bonds. Your tolerance for risk will be a factor in determining what kinds of investment to pursue. Higher risk investments, which have the potential for higher yield but perhaps some losses, may be more appropriate to the earlier years of your career. Many investors choose to mix less volatile investments into their portfolio as they approach retirement.

Housing in Retirement

Housing is one of the most important parts of retirement planning for clergy. If you have received housing support as part of your compensation and have used it to buy a home, you may have built up some equity that can be useful in either remaining in the home you have or in purchasing a new home. Clergy who have lived in church-provided housing will want to explore their housing options in some detail before retirement so that they can prepare.

There are a number of questions to consider as you look at housing in retirement. Where do you want to live? What are your priorities that will help you decide on location—proximity to family, climate, type of community, access to health care? What kind of housing would you like to live in? How much yard? How many floors? How much housing can you afford? Should you rent or buy?

Check with your denomination's staff to see what kind of tools they have for helping you weigh your options as you answer these questions. United Methodist clergy have access to online tools and financial planners through Wespath, their benefits administrator.

Housing Allowance in Retirement

In the previous clergy section, we covered the implications of the housing allowance that is offered to ministers. This allows ministers to exclude a housing allowance from income when they file federal income taxes. Fortunately, this benefit is also available to clergy in retirement.

The difference, for United Methodist clergy, is that instead of your local church making the official designation of the allowance, the annual conference is the designating body. The resolution making this designation is generally passed at the conference's annual session and is normally published in the conference journal. The resolution will usually designate 100 percent of your pension as a housing allowance.

In retirement, a housing allowance allows you to exclude from your income the smallest of these three amounts:

- the amount designated as a housing allowance by your annual conference,
- the amount spent for your qualified housing costs, such as mortgage, utilities, taxes, insurance, furnishings, and maintenance, or
- the fair rental value of your home, including furnishings, plus the current-year cost of your utilities.

As an active minister, your local church will not usually include the amount of the housing allowance on your W-2 (though it should be reported in Box 14 of the W-2 for transparency). But as a retired clergyperson, all of your distributions from your pensions body will be reported to the IRS, which means that it is the clergyperson's responsibility to exclude the housing allowance in your reported gross income.

One important circumstance should be noted with regard to this housing allowance benefit. A financial advisor who is unfamiliar with this provision may advise clergy to rollover their 403(b) tax-sheltered annuity plan into an IRA. If money at a church pension fund with a Private Letter Ruling (PLR) from the IRS is rolled over into a personal IRA, this significant housing allowance benefit is lost.

Another housing-related advantage to explore as a retired clergyperson is the implication of retaining a mortgage in retirement. In some cases, the principal and interest of the mortgage can lead to greater tax savings through the use of the housing allowance. Even though the idea of having a mortgage in retirement may not be attractive, you should investigate whether the tax savings from being able to exclude mortgage payments makes having the mortgage financially advantageous.

Health Care Costs and Long-Term Care Insurance

Another big factor in planning for retirement is the cost of health care. In a retirement planning document for clergy, Wespath reported that a typical 65-year-old couple retiring today without some sort of employer-sponsored health care will spend an average of $250,000 on medical care during retirement. Obviously, planning for such major expenses will have a major impact on your retirement.

A first place to start, if you are part of a denominational network, is consulting with your benefits officer to see if you have access to retiree health insurance. Check on the costs of such coverage and, if you are married, compare it to any retirement health insurance options your spouse may be entitled to. You'll also want to know how you qualify, what benefits are offered, and what limits there are on coverage.

Medicare is also a part of health care planning for retirement. This federal health insurance program is available to persons 65 and older who qualify for Social Security benefits. Most people should sign up for Medicare at age 65 if they are retired or retiring at that age. If they are still working and covered by a group health plan that will be primary before Medicare, they should only sign up for Medicare Part A at 65 and other parts when they retire. Retiree health plans generally are built on the expectation that those enrolled will also be enrolled in Medicare.

Outpatient prescription drug coverage is offered through Medicare for a monthly premium. You should consult with your retiree health insurance plan administrator to see if this coverage is offered in their plan.

Retirees may also purchase additional coverage to account for the gap between what Medicare actually pays and the associated expenses related to health care, such as deductibles, co-payments, and outpatient hospital services. Your benefits officer can tell you if a Medicare supplemental health insurance plan is available to you.

One big area that is not fully covered by Medicare or many health insurance plans is the cost of long-term care. Given the high costs associated with nursing home and home health care, having a plan to address these contingencies is important. Long-term care insurance can protect your savings and personal assets, which can quickly be eaten up to pay for this type of care. It can also give you options in what type of care you may be able to afford. A professional financial advisor can help you explore the costs of such plans and counsel you on how to proceed.

Social Security Benefits

Except for those rare clergy who have opted out of paying into self-employment Social Security taxes (see the previous clergy chapter), Social Security benefits remain a key part of a minister's retirement planning. The age at which persons could begin to receive the full Social Security benefit was 65 for many years. Recently it has been slowly rising. Persons born in 1955, for instance, will have to wait until they attain the age of 66 and two months before reaching full retirement age. For persons born in 1960 and later, the age will be 67.

You can check your estimated benefits on the Social Security website by setting up an account at https://www.ssa.gov/myaccount/. A retirement calculator can help you determine what you will be receiving and what the impact would be of delaying your benefits past your full retirement age. You can delay taking benefits until age 70 and your eventual Social Security retirement income will increase every month that you delay. This may be helpful in supplementing your overall retirement assets. If you are married, you will want to review the implications of how the income to you and your spouse would be affected by delaying benefits or taking them at full retirement age.

Other Factors in Planning for Retirement

As you assess your readiness for retirement, you may find that your projected resources are less than you hoped for. In those instances, you may want to consider some other options. One obvious way is to delay your retirement. The extra years of income from working can help you build up more savings while reducing your retirement years. The delay may also be beneficial to you as contributions to your pension plan continue, resulting in more years of service and potentially higher monthly payouts.

If you have other short-term sources of income, you might also consider delaying receipt of retirement benefits from some of your pension funds even after you officially retire. You are not required to begin monthly benefits until you reach the age of 72 or at the time of retirement, whichever is later. (You should also note that if you do not take the required monthly distribution when you meet the threshold, there is a 50 percent penalty.) In such scenarios, your retirement benefits could increase. They might also be reduced, however, so you should check with your pension administrator to see what the impact would be for you.

You should also check your budget, both the one you are using while working and the one you anticipate using in retirement. Using the tools in the other parts of this book, move toward a budget that allows you to spend less and save more during your working life. As you invest funds from your savings, they will have the chance to increase throughout your remaining working years.

Your retirement budget may also have room for changes. Moving to a smaller home or to a community with a lower cost of living may mean that you don't need all the income you hoped for. These budget decisions can contribute to a greater sense of financial freedom and may help your retirement years be more fulfilling.

Estate Planning

In the final clergy section, we will discuss how to approach conversations about estate planning with members of your congregation. It's also an important conversation for you to be having with the people you love and with professionals who can help you consider all the aspects of planning for your assets after your death. Financial planners, attorneys, insurance agents, and spiritual guides can help you determine what is important to you and how to best prepare your estate.

If you are married, one key consideration may be provision for a surviving spouse. Your spouse may have many retirement assets of his or her own, or your spouse may be more dependent on the resources you have accumulated through your working career. Doing a thorough review of your life insurance policies, both your own and those offered through your employers, is a good exercise to do before retirement.

You may want to offer support to children and grandchildren as well. One way to address this is by listing those you want to support as beneficiaries on your insurance policies and in any death benefits provided by your denomination. Periodic updates of your beneficiary forms will keep the names current.

You will also want to address the matter of survivor support in a last will and testament. Develop a relationship with a trusted attorney who can help you navigate this process. She or he can also advise you on methods to keep your financial information private following your death. This is useful to protect your surviving spouse and family members from unscrupulous actors who prey on the recently bereaved.

Financial planning with a professional, preferably someone with a with a CFP® (Certified Financial Planner) or ChFC® (Chartered Financial Consultant) designation, will also help you develop the right instruments to use in passing along your assets to the people and institutions you choose. Some of these instruments will help you avoid taxes that could reduce your bequest and can move your assets more quickly to their intended beneficiary. Explore whether trusts or endowment gifts may be helpful instruments for you.

Though we may sometimes think that we do not have much to offer to the causes that we love, endowments and bequests from even modest estates have blessed many churches and organizations through the years. In addition, designating a church or mission for memorial gifts upon your death gives others an opportunity to join in supporting something that is special to you. Be sure to discuss with your financial professional which of your assets would be most appropriate for churches and charities and which would be helpful for family members to receive. For instance, since charities are not required to pay taxes, they could receive funds that would otherwise carry tax liabilities, ultimately saving your heirs money.

One other consideration is the cost of your funeral arrangements and outstanding bills that you may leave. Have a conversation with a funeral home about your wishes so that the costs can be understood and planned for and so that your family members can be spared making difficult decisions at what will be a stressful time in their lives.

Documents for your Estate

Having prepared your estate, it is important to have all of your documents together and kept in a secure location that you have shared with trusted family members. Among the documents you should have are:

- A summary document that explains the other documents and the storage places of other key items referred to in them. This document may also include your funeral and burial plans.
- A draft obituar.y
- A contact list of the professionals who have assisted you with your estate planning, including attorneys, accountants, financial advisors, clergy, and funeral home.
- A copy of your will.

- A living will (or an Advanced Medical Directive), which directs physicians on the procedures you do and don't want to be performed if you are unable to make those decisions for yourself.

- A durable power of attorney for health care decisions. This document designates a loved one who will be able to make decisions about your care for you if you become unable to do so.

- A durable financial power of attorney. This is a similar document covering the management of your financial affairs.

Discussion Questions

- What insights do you find in the story of Ruth about planning for the future? What other biblical passages come to mind regarding retirement, saving, and planning for the future?

- How well do you understand the information on various considerations behind retirement planning? What did you learn in this section that stood out as especially useful?

- What obstacles exist for you, and for clergy in general, about saving for retirement? How do you navigate these obstacles?

- What unique opportunities do you have as a clergyperson regarding long-term savings and retirement, which non-clergy might not have?

- How do you currently feel about your preparation and planning for retirement?

- What are some steps you can take to improve your readiness for retirement?

- How do you talk to your congregation about retirement and estate planning?

- As you think about long-term savings and retirement for both yourself and your congregation, what stands out from this section as especially important or helpful? Why?

CHAPTER 5

Spending

It's so easy to spend. As payment technology has improved, one of the main goals of innovation has been to make the exchange of money as "friction-less" as possible. In addition to the convenience of credit cards, you can now pay online, through social media, with your phone, or with a smart watch. The interactions can be so fleeting that it hardly seems that you've done anything at all.

There's a danger in such ease, of course. With less friction the rub may come when you check your statements from the bank or credit card. You may find yourself asking, "How did I spend so much this month?"

Most of us don't want to dial back the convenience, but we can introduce more mindfulness about our spending. We'll be looking at some practical tools for doing that in this session. Mindfulness not only keeps us from spending beyond our means, it also helps us evaluate what's really important to us.

In one key episode in Jesus's ministry, a rich young man comes to Jesus with an important question. He wants to know what he has to do to inherit eternal life. As Mark tells it, Jesus saw how sincere this young man was. He really wanted to know the answer and "Jesus, looked at him carefully and loved him" (Mark 10:21). But then Jesus goes on to tell him a very hard thing. He knew that the young man's possessions were standing between him and a truly abundant life. So he tells him, "You are lacking one thing. Go, sell what you own, and give the money to the poor. Then you will have treasure in heaven. And come, follow me."

This was the kind of talk that made even the disciples, who had left everything, nervous. After this episode, Jesus took them aside and said, "It will be very hard for the wealthy to enter God's kingdom!" (v. 23).

This was too much for the disciples. They looked at each other and asked, "Then who can be saved?" (v. 26).

That's when Jesus reminded them that their desire to have things can be a distraction from an important spiritual message. Salvation is not ultimately about what we have or even what we can do. The thing the young man said he desired was about what God has done and is doing through grace. In Jesus's words: "It's impossible with human beings, but not with God. All things are possible for God" (v. 27).

Which is all just another way of saying what Jesus said in another teaching, "Stop collecting treasures for your own benefit on earth, where moth and rust eat them and where thieves break in and steal them. Instead, collect treasures for yourselves in heaven, where moth and rust don't eat them and where thieves don't break in and steal them. Where your treasure is, there your heart will be also" (Matthew 6:19-21).

What does a mindful spending practice look like? For John Wesley, who was given to deep examination of everything he did in life, having a set of questions helped him evaluate whether his use of money was helping him store up treasure where it counted. Wesley would probably have loved the idea of a book like the one you're reading right now. Wesley's questions, paraphrased below, went right back to the beliefs about money that we have discussed so far:

1. Am I acting as a steward of God's resources?

2. Am I living out of God's intentions as revealed in Scripture?

3. Can I offer up my actions with money as a sacrifice to God through Jesus Christ? and

4. Is this expense the kind of action that reflects love of God and neighbor?[1]

Buying a meal, with whatever form of payment you use, may not seem to raise important spiritual questions. After all, we have to eat. But we do pray, in the Lord's Prayer, "Give us this day our daily bread," indicating that even the provision of our most basic needs is a matter of relying on God and building our relationship with God.

However much you have in your bank account, you have been blessed by a God who wants the best for you. A God who, looking at you, loves you. Approaching our spending with mindfulness helps us see that love more clearly.

Activity: Getting Started

We've covered four of the five areas of our financial lives, so let's dive into the last (and maybe the hardest) one—Spending. Take a moment to think through your strengths and weaknesses when it comes to spending. What spending habits are you most proud of? Where do you know you could use some help?

Up until this point, we have focused on the concept of more—how we can give more, save more, and pay off more debt. Now we want to focus on less, how we can spend less while still providing adequately for our needs and the needs of those dependent upon us. This is the time when we try to find the money to help in our debt reduction efforts and to increase our giving and saving. This chapter will be about setting short-term goals for our spending categories and identifying some action steps to reduce expenses.

> ## WHAT OUR CONSUMER CULTURE SAYS ABOUT SPENDING
>
> - Things bring happiness.
> - Possessions define who we are.
> - The more we have, the more we should spend.
> - Spending is a competition.

As was true in the other four areas of our financial lives, spending is about more than just finances—it's about who you are and who you are becoming as a consumer.

Foolish   **Faithful**

The Consumer Culture   The Faithful Way

Let's start by taking a look at the pull of the consumer culture on the spender. There are four major messages that have influence on us:

- Things bring happiness.
- Your possessions define who you are.
- The more we have, the more we should spend.
- "Spending is a competition" (and the Joneses are the other team).

These statements are not entirely new to us since they are some of the myths and messages we've discussed throughout the study, but they all tend to converge on us in the area of spending.

Spending and the Faithful Way

In contrast to what our consumer culture is saying, the Bible calls us to be prudent in our spending. The prudent spender is one who enjoys the fruits of his or her labor yet guards against materialism.

Here we examine three biblical approaches related to our spending behavior. First, we are to beware of idols. In Deuteronomy 5:7-9, God self-identifies as a passionate God and commands that we have no other gods before God. Yet, since the beginning of time, we have wrestled with the temptation to replace God with other things. We've already said that, for many in our consumer culture today, the chief rival god is money. We ascribe godlike attributes to it. We think of it as being all-powerful, "the almighty dollar." We think of it as providing ultimate security. That's a false promise, but it's easy to understand the seduction of it.

> ## PRUDENT SPENDER
>
> One who enjoys the fruits of his or her labor yet guards against materialism.

What makes money an idol is our tendency to misplace our trust in God with trust in wealth, which is a dangerous condition as the Book of James warns, "Your riches have rotted. Moths have destroyed your clothes. Your gold and silver have rusted, and their rust will be evidence against you. It will eat your flesh like fire" (James 5:2-3). In contrast, God desires us to seek first the kingdom, and have faith that what we need will be given to us as well.

The second biblical approach is to guard against greed. We already looked at Luke 12:15, in which Jesus says, "Watch out! Guard yourself against all kinds of greed. After all, one's life isn't determined by one's possessions, even when someone is very wealthy." In contrast to greed, the Bible calls us to seek moderation. When the tribe of Israel was wandering in the desert, God provided manna to eat. But they could only collect enough for one day. If they took more, the rest would spoil.

Third, the Bible encourages us to have a sense of responsibility about what we have and to be generous and share with others less fortunate. In 1 Timothy, the members of an early Christian community are advised:

> *Tell people who are rich at this time not to become egotistical and not to place their hope on their finances, which are uncertain. Instead, they need to hope in God, who richly provides everything for our enjoyment. Tell them to do good, to be rich in the good things they do, to be generous, and to share with others. When they do these things, they will save a treasure for themselves that is a good foundation for the future. That way they can take hold of what is truly life. .*
>
> *1 Timothy 6:17-19*

Fourth, we're called to contentment. The apostle Paul explains in Philippians,

> *I know the experience of being in need and of having more than enough; I have learned the secret to being content in any and every circumstance, whether full or hungry or whether having plenty or being poor. I can endure all these things through the power of the one who gives me strength.*
>
> *Philippians 4:12-13*

SPENDING AND THE FAITHFUL WAY

- Beware of idols (Deuteronomy 5:7-9; James 5:2-3).
- Guard against greed (Luke 12:15).
- When we practice moderation and learn contentment, we are free to be generous and a blessing to others (1 Timothy 6:17-19).
- Contentment with and gratitude for what we have is the antidote to greed and envy (Philippians 4:12-13).

What this tells us is that contentment can be learned. Contentment with and gratitude for what we have is the antidote to greed and envy.

As we live into these biblical approaches and become prudent in our spending, we're reminded that God provides what we need. But we can't stop there.

Could it be that the greatest joy in what God has given us comes not from a quick fix of self-interest and immediate gratification but from being generous with God's resources and willing to share them with others?

A key motivation for growing in this area is knowing that when we practice moderation in our spending and learn contentment, we become free to be generous and a blessing to others.

> ## KEY QUESTION
>
> Are you willing to "claim your ground" in your spending lifestyle?

Claiming Your Ground in Spending

Understanding the challenge of being content in our circumstances and seeking moderation in our spending raises a key question: Are you willing, at some point, to claim your ground lifestyle-wise? What we mean by that question is a willingness to declare, "Enough is enough!" and to distinguish between your needs and your wants, between your true needs and what the consumer culture says you need.

> ## CLAIMING YOUR GROUND
>
> - Claiming your ground means you are willing to declare, "Enough is enough!"
> - When you claim your ground, you distinguish between your true needs and your wants (what the consumer culture says you need).

An example of this would be coming to a point where you would say, "You know, this house is big enough. It fits my needs. It keeps us warm in the winter and dry in the summer. Even if I make $10,000 a year, $50,000 a year, or $100,000 a year more and could afford a bigger house in a 'nicer' neighborhood, I'm not going to buy it. I don't need it." You could say the same thing about your car, or any other aspect of lifestyle that is challenging you to spend more than you know is reasonable.

As prudent spenders, the key question we need to ask ourselves is: When is enough, enough? Enough is about an attitude, not a numerical goal.

Activity: Claiming your Ground

Because this is such a key question, and because we're not often challenged to consider it, let's take a moment to think a little more about this concept of claiming our ground when it comes to spending. Spend some time in prayer and ask the Lord how you should answer the question: What would it mean for me to declare "Enough is enough" in my lifestyle?

My thoughts:

Categories of Spending

For the remainder of this chapter, we're going to go through the categories of your Spending Plan one by one and look a little deeper in each category.

It would be helpful to have your "What I Spend" worksheet from your pre-work handy as we go through each category.

Housing

Buying Versus Renting

For most of us, whether we own or rent, housing is the biggest expenditure we'll have in our lifetime. Notice that the first category on your Spending Plan under housing is mortgage/taxes/rent. There are several things to consider in this category.

First is the issue of renting versus owning. There's a commonly held belief that it's always better to own—that those who rent are just throwing money away. While there are many emotional and some financial advantages to owning a home, home ownership can also have financial disadvantages. Cost of home ownership is high. There are taxes, maintenance, additional utilities, and a host of other sometimes small, sometimes large, expenses that come with home ownership. And though most property values appreciate in value, that's not always a given.

Your personal circumstances may not be optimal for home ownership. Buying a home when there is a good chance you may move in two or three years does not make good financial sense. Flexibility is one of the advantages to renting. And if you have consumer debt or lack emergency savings, it's probably wiser to find an inexpensive rental and work on those areas before purchasing a home. If you lack the cash to make a reasonable down payment on a home, you'll be faced with extra costs like private mortgage insurance (PMI), which raises the amount of interest you will pay. Rather than taking on a mortgage that will potentially make you "house poor," meaning that your mortgage payments are so high that you have little left for other expenses, it would be wiser to rent inexpensively until you have saved enough for a larger down payment. As it turns out, there is something much worse than not owning a home—it's owning a home you can't afford. If you are considering buying versus renting, take a look at "To Buy or Not to Buy: Deciding to Rent or Purchase a Home" on page 150 of your Appendix.

Another point to consider when it comes to buying a home, if you have a partner, is whether you are basing your mortgage payment on one income or two incomes. Think back on what we discussed about handling two salaries. Though the mortgage companies will probably tell you differently, it is wise to be able to cover all your basic living costs with one income. If you are not able to do that now, think about waiting a few years to buy, and save money from the second income to make a bigger down payment that would enable you to pay your monthly mortgage on just one salary. If you feel you need to buy now, downsize your expectations and look for a home that can be managed with one income. That might sound strict, but consider: Is it worth some sacrifice and a bit of waiting to make the largest investment of your life more secure? (See "Financial Advantages of Buying a Smaller Home" on page 152 of your Appendix.)

Next, exercise extreme caution with regard to home equity loans, which are loans that allow you take out money (equity) that you have already paid into your mortgage. Home equity loans have become the ultimate credit card, used to fund people's desire to spend more than they make. To use a home equity loan to allow continued spending beyond your means is a trap that places your home in danger. Don't allow a home equity loan to be a means to fund short-term spending with long-term debt.

Maintenance and Repairs

If you're going to own a home, you'll save yourself a lot of money by learning basic repairs like fixing a dripping faucet and the importance of preventative maintenance tasks such as changing furnace and air conditioning filters and cleaning leaves out of gutters. Doing these things yourself greatly reduces expenses and prevents costly repairs later. There's lots of books and internet videos that can teach you the basics, or you can find a friend who is good at those kinds of things and ask for help or to trade services in some way.

Utilities

Another expense line on your Spending Plan under housing is utilities. There are lots of potential savings to look for in this category. One is controlling the thermostat. A couple degrees on the thermostat can make a significant difference in your heating and air conditioning bills. A programmable thermostat makes it easy to automatically have the settings change at night or times when you're gone.

In addition, make sure weather stripping and caulking are in good repair, replace bulbs with compact fluorescent or LED light bulbs, turn off lights, and minimize water usage. The month-after-month savings in utility costs can add up to be big savings over time.

Another place to evaluate your costs here are in phones and internet and cable services. Ask yourself whether you really need to pay for a land line. Shop for the latest and most cost-effective phone service packages and ask yourself what add-ons you really need. Many phone service providers offer group discounts for certain companies and organizations; see if you qualify for those savings. Take a close look at your plans to make sure you're really using the services you're paying for. Shop around and check out the various packages provided by internet service and/or cable providers. With cable or satellite, know that all companies have local basic plans that are much less expensive than the basic plan that's advertised. Another strategy is to call the provider and tell them you are interested in saving money or dropping services. Often times they have promotional deals or loyalty rates that they can offer you to stick with them.

For more tips, see "Saving on Utility Expenses" on page 152 of your Appendix.

MY SPENDING PLAN: HOUSING

1. Look at your pre-work worksheet "What I Spend" for what you currently spend for housing. (If you didn't complete the pre-work, use your best estimate of housing expenses. The percentage guidelines on the Spending Plan form can help guide you.)

2. Consider some of the issues discussed regarding housing (including maintenance and repairs and utilities). Write down at least one action step that you plan to take under this category.

   Action Step:

3. Set short-term goals for housing expenses, and fill in the Housing category of your Spending Plan worksheet, including the lines for Maintenance/Repairs and all Utilities.

Auto/Transportation

The next biggest expense category after housing is auto/transportation. No question about it, car expenses can eat you alive financially. But the good news is that the least expensive car you can drive is the one you already own. Keep it tuned up. Drive it sensibly. Make it last. (There is an exception to this rule: If you are currently driving a sports car made in Italy, a German-engineered luxury car, or any other car that carries a super high monthly payment, then it may be wise to consider ways to downsize to a more economical car.)

Sometimes people ask, "When is it economically wise to buy a new, never-owned car?" The answer is, "Never." We're not saying it's sinful to buy a brand-new, never-owned car. But from a purely financial standpoint, it's not the wisest thing to do because of the huge depreciation it will go through during the first two or three years, which may be 30 to 40 percent of the original cost of the car. See "A Big Difference in a Short Time: Buying a Used Car" on page 148 of your Appendix for more benefits of buying a used car.

Some people also question the economic advantage of leasing a car. Although you do pay less each month, you don't own anything at the end of the lease. However, a leased car may remain under warranty for the duration of the lease, and in some cases the lessee can emerge with equity in the vehicle. But there can be significant additional charges if you go over the mileage allocation or if wear and tear exceed what the dealer considers "normal," so it's not an ideal option for those who put significant miles on a car in a short period.

We recommend you keep and drive the car you have until it approaches the point that maintenance expenses exceed the value of the car. Generally, this happens at a much higher mileage level than most people expect. According to recent research the average reliable life of a new car is thirteen years and 145,000-plus miles. But the average time at which a new car is traded is a little more than four years and under 55,000 miles. Obviously, lots of folks are getting rid of their cars well before reliability becomes an issue. Again, buy used, treat it well, keep the fluids changed, and drive it for an extended period of time. If you do, you can pay cash for your next car.

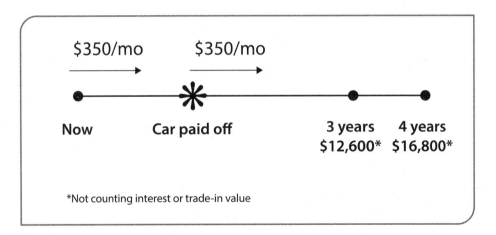

Let's assume you currently have a monthly car payment of $350. At some point, you'll pay the car off. What happens then? One of two things normally occurs. We might think, "The car is paid off, so it's time to get a new car." In that case, we are simply continuing the cycle of making car payments forever. Or the other thing that often happens is we say, "Great! The car is paid off. I'll keep it awhile longer and I now have $350 a month to spend on something else." But that makes no provision for when we will need to buy the next car.

Here's a better approach. When you get to the point of paying off your car, commit to keeping your car for another three or four years and continue the $350 per month payment to yourself. You've already been making the payments, so just continue doing what you have been. Put that amount into an interest-bearing account. Use direct deposit if possible. Let's look at what happens if you pay yourself for the next three or four years. By saving $350 a month, $4,200 a year, you'd have $12,600 at the end of three years, or $16,800 after four years. Plus you'd have a bit of interest and the trade-in value of your current car. You can pay cash for your next car.

And if you keep that next car for six to eight years, keep putting money into your replacement savings. The amount can conceivably be lower than it was before, perhaps $200, because you have a longer time horizon to save for the next car. And the difference between what you were saving and what you're now saving, that $150 can go to meeting one or more of your financial goals.

Also, don't forget about getting the most out of your gas mileage. See "How to Get the Most Out of Every Tank of Gas" on page 149 of your Appendix.

MY SPENDING PLAN:
AUTO/TRANSPORTATION

1. Look at your pre-work worksheet "What I Spend" for what you currently spend in Auto/Transportation category. (If you didn't complete the pre-work, use your best estimate of expenses. The percentage guidelines on the Spending Plan form can help you.)
2. Consider any ways you can reduce these expenses. Write down at least one action step you plan to take.

    Action Step:

3. Set goals for these categories and fill in your Spending Plan form.

Insurance

The next category on your Spending Plan form is Insurance, one of the least understood and least monitored areas of personal finances. *Catastrophic* is the key word for insurance. Insurance exists to protect you from a major or a catastrophic loss.

Auto Insurance

When it comes to auto insurance, choose the plan with the highest deductible you can afford. The deductible is the amount you pay in case of an accident. Plans with higher deductibles will have a lower monthly payment. The lower the deductible, the higher the cost of the insurance. The key is to have an emergency fund in place. If you would be able to pay $1,000 in case of an accident, don't get a policy with a $500 deductible.

Although paying $1,000 rather than $500 in the event of an accident is unfortunate, it would be worth it if premium savings added up to more than that over a few years. In that same vein, consider eliminating collision coverage on an older car. If you have enough in your car replacement savings to replace your car if it gets totaled, then you can drop your collision coverage, which is the most expensive part of your policy.

Second, shop around for auto insurance. Often there are significant differences between companies in terms of rates, coverage, and service. Various websites provide comparative rate information. Check with a rating service like A. M. Best to be sure the company is sound. Another way to save money is to combine policies when possible. For example, combining auto and homeowner's insurance and having all cars on one policy usually results in significant discounts. Look for other discounts, too. Most companies offer discounts for good students, good drivers, and cars with certain safety features and low mileage.

Life Insurance

As we mentioned earlier, we believe that we are called to provide for those who are dependent on us. Part of the way to provide for them is to have insurance in the event that something happens to you as a principal wage earner. But the common problem is that when we need life insurance the most, we can afford it the least. We need it most when our families are young and, generally speaking, our income is the lowest and our expenses are high. (The good news is life insurance is cheapest when you're young.) In the vast majority of situations, renewable term insurance is your best option. It provides maximum coverage for the minimum premium.

WHOLE VS. TERM LIFE INSURANCE

Term life insurance covers you for a fixed period, ten, twenty, or thirty years, for example, and pays benefits if you die during that time. Whole life insurance covers you until you die, and the money you pay into it builds a cash value that you can access later in life.

However, life insurance may not be necessary for you. If you are single with no dependents, or if your children are grown and on their own, assets have accumulated, or if both spouses have the ability to earn significant income, in those cases, you may not need life insurance except perhaps as part of an overall estate plan. Given the variety of insurance products available, it's a good idea to consult with one or two trusted professionals prior to making this kind of decision.

Two other notes about life insurance. First, consider disability insurance. Disability income insurance is very important and the good news is it's not expensive. If you are not covered through an employer, you need to have disability as part of your insurance plan. Second, you may want to consider long-term care insurance. As we grow older, health problems requiring a nursing home or in-home care can create major financial problems. There are lots of pros and cons to long-term care insurance but as you enter your fifties, it may be wise to investigate this type of insurance.

MY SPENDING PLAN: INSURANCE

1. Look at your pre-work worksheet "What I Spend" for what you currently spend on the insurance categories. (If you didn't complete the pre-work, use your best estimate of expenses. The percentage guidelines on the Spending Plan form can help you.)

MY SPENDING PLAN: INSURANCE

2. Consider any ways you can reduce these expenses. Write down at least one action step you plan to take.

   Action Step:

3. Set goals for these categories and fill in your Spending Plan form.

Household/Personal, Entertainment, and Professional Services

Next up are Household/Personal, Entertainment, and Professional Services. These categories are often hard to control but making your plan now will help you get a handle on these expenses.

MY SPENDING PLAN: HOUSEHOLD AND PERSONAL EXPENSES

1. Fill in an amount that you'd like for the Small Cash Expenditures category, if you have not already. This is for small items like coffee or food you might pick up throughout the day.

2. Look at your pre-work for what you currently spend on Household/Personal, Entertainment, and Professional Services. If you didn't complete the pre-work "What I Spend" worksheet, use your best estimates of expenses. The percentage guidelines on the Spending Plan form can help you.

3. Next, select three or four categories you think have the most potential to be reduced, and read the information on the following pages (90–100) pertaining to these expenses. Write down at least one idea that can help you reduce expenses in each of those categories and write those goals for each on your Spending Plan form.

MY SPENDING PLAN: HOUSEHOLD AND PERSONAL EXPENSES

4. Set goals for all remaining categories and enter them on your Spending Plan form.

5. Review your entire form and if there are categories that you have not already completed, do so now.

6. Total all your expenses and fill out the box in the lower right corner of your Spending Plan form.

   (At this time, don't be concerned about whether the income and expenses balance. We will address this in the next chapter.)

Household/Personal Expenses

Groceries

Groceries can be a budget buster. Government statistics show a major difference between the amount spent on a monthly basis by families that are thrifty spenders versus lavish spenders. Almost twice as much is spent on food by the lavish shoppers. This is a key area of the budget to examine.

Here are a variety of tips for reducing your grocery bill:

- Make a list—and stick to it (perhaps the single most effective way to control food costs).

- Use coupons.

- Buy private label or store brands.

- Considering buying bulk where there are cost savings.

- Shop at discounted food stores.

- Beware of marketing techniques that encourage impulse purchases.

- Make up a price list on common items so you can recognize a good deal when you are shopping.

- Remember that convenience foods cost more.

- Buy fruits and vegetables in season and check out local farmers markets if available.

- Plant a vegetable garden.

- Eliminate or reduce snack foods.

- Planning meals for a week or more in advance (particularly in conjunction with advertised sales) and freezing for future use saves money and time on both purchase and preparation.

- Saving money on food does not mean sacrificing nutritional value. In fact, many of the items that are comparatively most expensive (snack foods, sugared cereals, soft drinks) have the least nutritional value. You can eat inexpensively and healthfully.

Clothes/Dry Cleaning

Clothing can be a very emotional area for many people. Sometimes we buy clothes we don't need just to feel better about ourselves or we pay exorbitant prices because we feel our self-worth is based on what we wear. If you sense that's true about you, we encourage you to seek help in getting to the bottom of those feelings. God doesn't want you to evaluate your worth by what you wear.

If you are a parent, beware of reinforcing the cultural message to your children that their value is based on what they wear by overspending on brand-name clothing for them.

Here's some startling statistics:

- Ten percent of clothing gets worn 90 percent of the time.
- One-third of clothing never gets worn.

These statistics may be because we bring new clothes home and they don't look the same under our lighting as they did in the store, they don't match an outfit the way we thought they would, they don't fit quite right, or we just didn't need them in the first place. It's amazing how few clothes one could really get by on. If you had three pairs of pants, three shirts, and three pieces of outerwear like jackets or sweaters, and if they mixed and matched, you could have twenty-seven different outfits. In fact, a current trend is the "capsule wardrobe" that is based on just that concept: a small supply of basic clothing items that mix and match to make a variety of outfits. And how many pairs of shoes do we really need? See "Resisting the Urge to Purchase" on page 147 for more on this.

The point is, buy sensibly. Buy classic styles that won't quickly go out of fashion and look for ways to mix and match color schemes. One experiment might be to somehow tag your clothing at the beginning of the season and, at the end of the season, see which items have not been worn and consider giving those away.

Here are some additional tips on clothing:

- Challenge yourself to make it through a season change without buying new clothes unless absolutely necessary.
- Buy during the off-season for better deals.
- Shop at discount stores and consignment shops, both online and in person.
- Welcome hand-me-downs.
- Buy non-name brand clothing.
- Trade outgrown children's clothes with other families.
- Shop rummage and garage sales for children's clothing.
- Buy fabrics that don't require expensive dry cleaning.

Gifts

Perhaps you were surprised by how much gifts add up when you did your gift list in the pre-work. Gifts can be a significant item in the Spending Plan, one that we don't always consider. And the ironic thing is that we often are creating financial stress for ourselves by buying gifts for folks who already have everything they need and a lot more besides. The key principle is that the cost of the gift is not a reflection of your love. Remember that not only are the best things in life free, the best things in life aren't things.

There are lots of ideas for reducing your gift expenditures:

- Make a gift list.
- Have a gift budget.
- Make or bake gifts.

- Invite people for a special meal instead of buying a gift.

- Write a letter of appreciation to the person (what you really appreciate about that person and your relationship to her or him) rather than buying a gift.

- Give to a charity in a person's name. The money goes where it's really needed, and the person knows he or she has been thought of (and you may even get a tax break).

- Give coupons for doing things for someone like chores, backrubs, or manicures.

- Shop at low-cost stores. Dollar stores are good choices for inexpensive children's gifts.

- Make agreements between families to limit the amount spent and the number of persons to whom gifts are given. Draw names from a hat to determine whom you'll give to.

- Be on the lookout for appropriate gifts year-round so you can get them when on sale.

- Save on the cost of greeting cards: Buy next year's cards right after this year's holiday, or purchase cards from dollar stores. Or make your own.

Books/Magazines/Music/Other Subscriptions

Two important questions to ask yourself when it comes to items in this category:

1. Do you actually read, watch, or listen to it? The cheapest subscription or sale price in the world is still not a bargain if we never get around to reading or listening to the material.

2. The second question may be more important than the first. *Should* you read, watch, or listen to the material? Take to heart these words: "From now on, brothers and sisters, if anything is excellent and if anything is admirable, focus your thoughts on these things: all that is true, all that is holy, all that is just, all that is pure, all that is lovely, and all that is worthy of praise" (Philippians 4:8).

The following ideas may help you save money in this category:

- Use the library—get a return on your taxes. Libraries offer ebooks, audio books, and magazines free of charge. Libraries sometimes have free tickets to local concerts and cultural events as well.

- Buy paperbacks instead of hardcover books.

- Read websites instead of hard copies of magazines or newspapers.

- Buy used books online.

- Consider audio subscription services as an alternative to buying music online or in stores.

- Monitor subscriptions to streaming platforms or other services based on automatic payments to make sure you are actually using them and want to continue.

Allowances

Age four or five is not too young for children to learn the basic biblical principles for handling their money, but for children to learn to handle money wisely, they must have some with which to work. Allowances can be the means by which they receive money and can be an excellent teaching tool.

Here's a technique to use with small children. Plan a time each month to sit down with your children and talk about their allowance. You might give your children their allowance in dimes to help break down the concept of dollars. Give each of them a series of paper cups. On each cup, write what the cups represent. For instance, one might be labeled "Giving" and the first dime of every dollar could be placed in that cup. Discuss why we give to God as you explain the cup. A second cup might be labeled "Savings" and the second dime of each dollar could go here. Again this invites discussion of why we save. Another cup might go for "Gifts." Lastly, there can be a cup for whatever they want to use the money for—"Spending." As your children grow older they can graduate to more advanced tools like a written budget with categories for things like school lunch and gym shoes. In high school they can transition into covering their own expenses out of their earnings and use budgeting software to keep on target.

Other families have used similar ideas and given their children three banks, one each for giving, saving, and spending. Each bank received a portion of any money the child obtained.

Personal Technology

With technology changing so rapidly, it is easy to get caught up in the "need" to have the latest and greatest new development. However, if you don't really need it, having the latest technology can be a costly venture. Consider the following hints to hold down costs in this area:

- Think about purchasing refurbished computers, cameras, or phones, instead of new. Some items marked "refurbished" are actually brand new; they were simply returned by people who decided they didn't want them. And refurbished items often must pass the strictest performance inspections just to be sold again under the manufacturer's name. These can be great buys.

- Avoid the most expensive offerings. Often the highest-end models include features most people rarely use. For example, computers with a slightly slower processor come with a substantial price discount and little or no observable reduction in performance.

- Recognize that even if your technology is no longer state-of-the-art, if it still adequately performs the tasks you bought it for, you don't "need" to upgrade. Much of the marketing for technology products blurs the line between needs and wants.

- See if the organization you work for will buy the device for you if it aids you in your work. If not, look into writing it off at tax time.

- Take the time to research your purchase once you determine that you will benefit from that piece of technology. Look for websites to get third-party and owner reviews. Use price comparison websites to get the lowest prices.

- Take a pass on the extended warranty. These are seldom worth the cost.

Education

Precollege

For a variety of reasons, some of us struggle with the decision of private versus public school for our children. This is a very sensitive, even volatile, topic. It is mentioned here because of the financial implications of that decision.

In making the decision, recognize that the number one influence on our children's development is what takes place in the home. In light of that, a foremost goal should be to ensure that the environment of the home is protected. Thus, an important question is whether sending your children to private school will put you into a debt situation. If the answer is yes, and considering the stress that debt causes on a family, it would be difficult under those circumstances to justify paying for private education. This is not an anti-private education statement; it is simply speaking to a financial reality. If you are set on private education, look in your Spending Plan and determine what other sacrifices you are willing to make to fund that education without placing financial stress upon the family.

College

If you want to help your children financially with their college education, start saving early. Allow the cumulative effect of compound interest to work for you and receive tax advantages by saving in a 529 College Savings Plan or a Coverdell Education Savings Account. Early on, share with your children that they have a responsibility to assist with their college expenses through money they begin saving in middle school or earlier. Set the goal of having no college debt after graduation. Set the expectation of working ten to fifteen hours per week while in college. No curriculum is so difficult that a student cannot work ten to fifteen hours a week and still have time to study and socialize. That, combined with full-time vacation and summer work, can easily generate $5,000 to $10,000 a year toward expenses.

Some further ideas for reducing college costs include:

- Opt for a state university. You may think your child needs an Ivy League education in order to be successful. However, only a few of the CEOs at the top 500 companies graduated from such schools. Most went to state universities or to less-known private colleges.[2]

- By all means be diligent in exploring scholarships but beware of offers to help you find scholarships for a fee (sometimes hundreds of dollars). Such assistance often amounts to referral of potential scholarship sources that a little effort on your part can uncover.

- Attend a two-year college and then transfer to a four-year institution. The cost of the first two years will be much lower—in addition to the potential savings of living at home those two years. The student's degree will still be from the four-year school. Be sure the four-year school the student plans to attend accepts credits from the two-year school.

- Take part in a cooperative program that alternates periods of study with work experience in which the student can earn a significant portion of the next period's tuition.

- Work a year before college. Gain experience and maturity as well as save funds for college.

- Serve in the military and use government grants to then pay for college.

- Be cautious about student loans. It has become a common assumption that student loans are a good thing—a low-interest way to finance an education. While interest rates for student loans do tend to be favorable, they are still a form of debt and must be repaid. Too often young people start life with loans totaling tens of thousands of dollars—a huge financial burden with which to begin adult life. Some college advisors and financial aid officers counsel that tuition should not figure into the decision of where to attend. Their line of reasoning is that the higher the cost, the more financial aid the student will qualify for. But the fact that often goes unmentioned is that 85 percent of student financial aid comes in the form of loans (that's a nice way of saying *debt*). The relative cost of a given college should logically be a factor in the decision of where to attend. Some loans may be necessary, but carefully consider alternatives that minimize loans as you plan for college expenses. It's possible (and preferable!) to complete college without a loan.

Entertainment: Going Out

Entertainment is much more enjoyable if you are not anxious about how you will pay for it. Consider the following options for spending less on this category:

- Go out to your favorite expensive restaurant, but go for dessert only. Enjoy the ambiance at a fraction of the cost.
- Order tap water with a slice of lemon rather than drinks. The difference in your final bill can be substantial.
- Go to matinee or second-run movies, or wait for them to come out online
- Pack lunches and snacks when going on family outings.
- Trade babysitting duties with another family.
- Take advantage of free or low-cost local attractions—free days at museums, park district offerings, library programs.
- Entertain friends in your home. Enjoy a potluck meal together. Play board games. Rediscover how both your relationships and your bank accounts can grow from doing so.
- Walks in the park and drives in the country can provide times of good conversation, relaxation, and, in the case of walking, some good exercise.

Entertainment: Travel

With the costs of transportation, lodging, and meals on the rise, travel expenses and vacations must be carefully planned for and budgeted, or their costs lowered by seeking less expensive alternatives. An important question is: Are two weeks of expensive fun worth fifty weeks (or more!) of anguish over how to pay for it?

Some tips for lowering vacation costs include:

- Take shorter trips.
- Travel in the off-season.
- Stay with friends or relatives to save on hotel costs.

- Cut food costs by taking food along, traveling with a cooler in the car, and staying where breakfast is included in the cost (or at least, where children eat free).

- Try camping. It is the experience most often cited as the most cherished childhood memory. See if you can borrow and share equipment with friends. There is no need for all of us to own a tent and other equipment we use only a few times a year.

- Understand that it is not the birthright of every child to go to expensive destinations like Disney World, nor is it an essential experience for their normal growth and development. If such an experience can fit within your Spending Plan, good. If not, be assured that your child will be better served by your not suffering the effects of the resultant debt.

Entertainment: Other

The "Other" area under Entertainment contains several expenses. A major expense (under Fitness/Sports) can be membership at a fitness center. Care of our bodies is part of biblical stewardship. The question is, do you actually use the membership? Even if you do, consider if there is a less expensive way to stay in shape. Basic exercises at home, a good walking program, and wise eating may be all that's necessary.

Hobbies are quite legitimate and good for our psychological well-being. But because we tend to really enjoy our hobbies, the money spent on them can easily get out of hand. Buy used equipment for your hobbies and sports. Build hobby expenses into the Spending Plan and then stick with it. If your hobby is too expensive, find a less expensive alternative.

Professional Services

Childcare

No one would advocate anything but the very best childcare. Obviously, working single parents need some form of childcare, and the monthly cost of childcare can sometimes exceed any other household expense, including housing.

But married parents have the opportunity to evaluate whether both parents working and paying for childcare is the best use of their income. Financially, the spendable income from the second salary may not warrant the sacrifice made after subtracting the costs, both perceived and actual, of maintaining a two-income household.

For most people, childcare is not optional. When choosing a childcare provider, consider whether your schedule is flexible and you can make do with a less expensive four- or three-day option. Many providers offer discounted rates for partial weeks. Some childcare centers even offer full or partial scholarships based on income, so be sure to explore that option if you qualify.

Activity: Wrapping Up

1. What is the best idea you got from reading the cost-saving material in your workbook?

2. Complete any remaining part of your Spending Plan that you've been unable to until now.

CHAPTER 6

Adjusting the Spending Plan

We began this study by talking about the constant anxiety that our fears about money can bring. Rather than ignoring those fears, our study has led us to confront them directly and you now have some new tools for approaching your financial life. Hopefully, you are beginning to gain confidence that growing in this area is also a way of growing closer to God.

We've established that Jesus had a lot to say about money, but he also had some things to say about worry. In one much-quoted passage of the Gospel of Luke, Jesus tells his disciples, "Don't worry about your life, what you will eat, or about your body, what you will wear. There is more to life than food and more to the body than clothing" (Luke 12:22-23).

There is a difference between attention and worry. Worry eats away at our awareness that we are dependent on God, who desires the best for us. Attention does the opposite. When we pay attention to the ways God works in the world and in our lives, we see possibilities for a richer, fuller life that we can't see when worry clouds our vision.

I think this is why Jesus goes on in this passage to talk about birds and flowers. "Consider the ravens," he says: "they neither plant nor harvest, they have no silo or barn, yet God feeds them. You are worth so much more than birds!" (Luke 12:24).

"Notice how the lilies grow," Jesus goes on to say. "They don't wear themselves out with work, and they don't spin cloth. But I say to you that even [the great king] Solomon in all his splendor wasn't dressed like one of these. If God dresses grass in the field so beautifully, even though it's alive today and tomorrow it's thrown into the furnace, how much more will God do for you, you people of weak faith!" (vv. 27-28).

Of course, Jesus knew that we need to be fed and clothed, but he chose these simple examples to remind us that we are not alone or without resources. God does provide abundantly and gifts us with wisdom, work, and community to receive what we need. We will understand ourselves better if we pay attention to how God cares for the rest of creation.

Something happens when we pay attention. A poet describing a simple scene or moment will discover dimensions to it that can open our eyes and even change our lives. When we pay attention to our finances, even through the diligent work of keeping records, we can see things we never saw before and begin to see how God works through our attention. When we lay out in a document the things we are spending our money on, we can begin to see the things that are important to us, and perhaps the things that we say are important really receive very little of our budget.

John Wesley was a dedicated journaler who kept copious records of his income and expenses. He made a similar account of his spiritual life, noting the ways he had participated in prayer, worship, and study each day. Like the Enlightenment scientists of his time, Wesley believed that this kind of careful observation could help him grow in his understanding and faith.

He was right about that and the practice still holds true. When we are careful about recording our income and expenses and careful about attending to our relationship with God, we do grow in understanding and faith. We also grow more trusting that God will use this work to help us live more freely and abundantly.

In another one of Jesus's stories, he talks about a man going on a journey who gave his servants his property to oversee. They received differing amounts of money, but two of the servants shepherded the money into a profit while the third buried his in the ground, fearing that his master would be angry if he lost any of it.

When the man returned, he praised the two who took special care to steward the resources they had been given into growth. He chastised the fearful servant

102   ■   Saving Grace

and told the other two, "Well done! [or Excellent!] You are a good and faithful servant!" (Matthew 25:21, 23; read entire story in vv. 14-30). This story helps us see the God who does not want us to operate from fear, but gives us confidence that our efforts will bear fruit.

Activity: Getting Started

What cost-saving practices were you able to put into effect this past week?

Congratulations! You now have the first draft of your Spending Plan completed. It's time now to help you refine your Spending Plan to better fit your financial goals. Now is also a great time to revisit your pre-work, fill in more information, and make adjustments where necessary.

Now that you are able to see your income in comparison to your total expenses, you will see one of three possible scenarios:

1. Your income equals your expenses.

2. Your income exceeds your expenses.

3. Your expenses exceed your income.

If your income equals your expenses, you have a balanced Spending Plan, which is a good place to be. Scenario two is even better—your income exceeds your expenses.

For many of us, we will find ourselves in scenario three, where our expenses still exceed our income. This is not exactly exciting news, but don't be discouraged. Take a deep breath. Trust in God to help you through. Pray for guidance, and remember, you can do this!

Prioritizing the Four Uses of Money

Before we get into the details of how you'll adjust your plan, let's take a moment to talk about how to prioritize our money. Let's start with a question that affects us all: If giving is so right and saving is so wise and staying out of debt is preferable and controlling our spending makes us good stewards, why are they so hard to do?

Part of the answer lies in the way we approach the four uses of money—giving, saving, incurring debt, and spending. It's easy to choose a lifestyle first and spend accordingly. We get this job, and a certain annual income, and we ask, "Where do I want to live? What sort of car do I want to drive? How do I want to have fun? What kind of clothes do I want to wear?"

Given our natural tendencies and the powerful pull of the consumer culture, when we begin with lifestyle, we end up using all our income there. And if we use all our income for lifestyle, we will wind up in debt. Because even if our spending stays within our income, if we're not building up savings, the first time an unexpected expense happens, the bill winds up on the credit card and we begin to spiral down into debt. Now our lifestyle is taking all the income and there is still debt to pay off.

In that situation, saving and giving end up last on the list. With debt payments and lifestyle expenses, there's simply no way to save or be generous. There is nothing left.

So let's look at a different order for the things we can do with money, which begins with God's intentions in mind. That order is giving, saving, then lifestyle.

First, we decide how much to give. That will be the initial amount we pay each pay period, according to the concept of first fruits giving. Second, we decide how much to save, and we save that amount right off the top as well. The easiest way to do that is through direct deposit from an employer right into a

PRIORITIZING MONEY

- Consumer culture says spend on lifestyle first, and then give and save.
- The faithful way is to give first, then save, then consider lifestyle spending.

TRANSITIONING OUT OF DEBT

- Give something.
- Save something.
- Aim for maximum repayment of debt.
- Minimize lifestyle spending to maximize funds available for debt repayment.

savings account. Third, based on what is left after giving and saving, we establish our lifestyle. Now we decide where we can afford to live, what kind of car we can afford to drive, how much we'll spend on clothing, entertainment, and the rest. If we approach how we use our money in that order, there's not going to be a fourth item—debt—to contend with. We won't have debt because we will have emergency savings for the unexpected.

You may be saying, "Great in theory and it sounds good, but what if a person is already in consumer debt? What do they do now? How do they get to the place of handling money in the right order?" If that's your situation, there is a transitional phase. We still start with giving and saving. Then we address debt and spending.

Transitioning Out of Debt

While you're in the transitional phase, the word associated with giving is *something*. When we talked about giving we said that there's no excuse for not giving *something*. At this point, it may not be a whole lot, but it should be something based on gratitude for what we have, not discontent for what we don't have. Don't miss out on the joy of giving, even during transitional times, and on the blessings that come from God as we open up in faith. Next, begin to save and the word is again, *something*.

As long as we have debt, we may not save very much, because our key priority is to accelerate debt repayment. At the same time, we do want to begin the saving habit. Our emergency savings is what will ultimately prevent future debt when the unexpected happens. A good starting goal is to save $500 or $1,000 as soon as possible and grow from there. The key is to start saving *something*. Adjust your Spending Plan to where you are now, or where you can reasonably stretch yourself in the next month or two to add to your savings. See if you can adjust any of your expenses to help reach that goal.

The final consideration is lifestyle, and the word associated with lifestyle in the transitional phase is *spartan*. By *spartan* we mean living a frugal life, with fewer frills and luxury, and using self-control and willpower to do so. This means taking short-term and sometimes drastic steps to minimize spending in order to maximize funds available for debt repayment and emergency savings. For example, let's say we're currently spending $100 a month on entertainment, and we commit for the next six months to spending only $15 a month for entertainment. We Netflix and chill with microwave popcorn instead of spending $50 or $60 at the movie theater (basic Netflix is $9/month, but of course we could DVR and chill!). We take a walk in the park, have friends over for potluck dinner, or do game nights and play board games to replace expensive activities. These activities often provide much better opportunities for deepening our relationships with friends and family, as well as saving a good amount of money.

The $85 difference between what we were spending on entertainment and the $15 we now spend goes to debt repayment and emergency savings. Similarly, for clothes, instead of currently spending $120 a month, we commit to $25 for the absolute necessities. We commit to wearing last year's wardrobe when the seasonal change comes, or shopping at secondhand stores or websites when we need something new. Most of us could do that very easily and still look very nice. The $95 dollars saved again goes toward debt and emergency savings. Add the $85 from entertainment and the $95 from clothing and you already have an extra $180 dollars toward debt repayment and savings.

Living a spartan lifestyle involves looking at all the categories of the Spending Plan and finding every area where short-term cutbacks can be made to take a big step toward debt repayment. Remember this is a season, not the rest of your life.

If you are in this transitional phase, it will be a challenge, but the payoff—debt reduction—will definitely be worth it.

HOW TO BRING INCOME AND EXPENSES INTO BALANCE

1. Increase income.
   But simply increasing income does not deal with the root problem of why expenses exceed income.
2. Sell assets to pay off some debt.
   This may be wise but also does not deal with the root problem.
3. Reduce expenses to live within your existing income.
   Do I have optional expenses I can eliminate?
   Do I have variable expenses I can further reduce?
   Can I eliminate any assumptions about "fixed" expenses?

How to Bring Income and Expenses into Balance

If your Spending Plan is out of balance, there are three main strategies you can use to get your finances back in order.

Increase Income

First, you can increase income. You or your spouse, if you're married, could get an additional job. In a few cases, doing this for a short time may be helpful. However, simply increasing income does not deal with the root issue of why spending is exceeding income in the first place. Until those reasons have been addressed, more income will probably only lead to more spending and not solve the problem. In addition, after factoring in taxes, additional expenses of travel, clothing, less time to carefully shop, or more meals out or preprepared, the additional net income can be very little, not to mention the impact of increased fatigue and less personal time.

That said, in today's gig economy, it is easy and efficient to pick up extra work. If this is an option, one strategy might be earmarking any additional income solely for debt reduction or building emergency savings. Delivering takeout or groceries, providing ride-share, or freelancing in your skill area might accelerate the cumulative process of debt repayment or increase savings for more security in the long run. Wesley was a believer in industrious, honest work, in "gaining all you can" so that you might be freed up from money concerns and be able to in turn give all you can. Let your personal situation guide you to increase your income in ways that address current problems rather than creating new ones.

Sell Assets

The second way to bring the plan into balance is to sell assets to pay off some debt. Perhaps you have some things you no longer use or need that can be sold. That's a short-term approach that can give you a jumpstart toward balancing your Spending Plan by allowing you to pay down your debt and may be a very wise thing to do. But again, it doesn't get to the root of the problem of why spending is exceeding income. If that doesn't change, the debt will build back up and you'll be right back where you started—minus an asset.

Reduce Expenses

The final way to bring the plan into balance is to reduce expenses. The key is to live within existing income. To do this, look very carefully once again at each expense category on your Spending Plan, and ask yourself the following questions, in this order:

1. "Do I have optional expenses I can eliminate?" Good places to look for these are in the household and entertainment categories. I know some of you may be saying, "I don't have any optional expenses," but here's the truth: streaming services are optional; television is optional; eating out is optional; most clothing purchases are optional.

2. "Do I have variable expenses I can further control and reduce?" Look at utilities, groceries, and other household items. What about a further adjustment to the thermostat? How about shopping at a lower-cost grocery store? Could you stop buying coffee out every day? Where are there variable expenses you can further control and reduce in your Spending Plan?

3. "Can I eliminate any assumptions about 'fixed' expenses?" Costs like mortgage or rent and car payments are "fixed" only if we continue to live where we live and drive what we drive. We may need to consider downsizing our living situation or renting out a room. Is there a way to eliminate the "fixed" cost of two cars by finding a creative way to get by with one?

4. "How serious am I about this?" Are you underestimating the long-term pain and consequences of not getting your financial house in order now? Sometimes it may just mean giving up something you really enjoy for a while. Trust God and look forward to what blessings may be found during a time of simplicity.

MY SPENDING PLAN: MAKING ADJUSTMENTS

Let's take some time now to adjust your Spending Plan.

If your income equals or exceeds your expenses, follow the instructions under part A below. If your expenses exceed your income, follow the instructions under part B.

A. If income equals or exceeds expenses, prayerfully and carefully review all categories to see if you can increase that margin even further. Are there any areas where you can cut back your expenses? If so, reflect on how that margin (extra money) can best be used to further your goals.

Write down at least one action step you plan to take and make any adjustments to your Spending Plan form.

Action Step:

B. If your expenses exceed your income, prayerfully and carefully review all the categories of your Spending Plan to see where you can reduce expenses, asking the questions we discussed around reducing expenses. Write down at least one action step (but you may need to do a few) that you plan to take to adjust your Spending Plan. Then, adjust the plan and bring it into balance as best you can.

Action Step:

Moving Forward with the Plan: Record Keeping

Now that you've done the hard work of coming up with a balanced Spending Plan, let's talk about how to keep yourself on track as you move forward.

First, it's important to keep records because it gives us accurate data, which tells us if and how we need to adjust our Spending Plan. Right now, your Spending Plan is theoretical. Some of the numbers are what you really spend, others are what you think you spend, and some are goals. We need accurate information on what really takes place. Were our assumptions correct? Are our goals realistic?

> ## BENEFITS OF RECORD KEEPING
>
> - Gives accurate data.
> - Improves family communication and single contentment.
> - Allows for midcourse corrections.
> - Provides a form of accountability.

Second, record keeping improves communication among couples and families, as well as contributes to a sense of well-being for singles.

Third, record keeping allows midcourse corrections. If circumstances change and your actual expenses are higher or lower than you planned, you will have the information to make the adjustments.

Finally, keeping records provides a form of accountability. Often we're not aware how the simple act of record keeping will impact our spending behavior simply as a daily reminder of our goals and commitment and how well we're doing. This is key to staying on track.

There are three record-keeping systems we recommend: using the envelope system, keeping written records, or using a digital platform.

Envelope System

Next, let's look at the envelope system. Perhaps you'll recognize a form of this system used by many of our grandparents and great-grandparents. Maybe they used a variety of containers—a coffee tin here and a sugar bowl there. One container held money for groceries, one for clothing, and another for a rainy day. When a purchase was considered, they looked into the appropriate container and determined what could or could not be spent based on how much money was in it. It was a very tangible way to designate money for various expenses.

The envelope system is based on the same principle. Here is how it works. Take a look at the illustration below. On the left-hand side you'll see how, in theory, you deposit all your income into a master bank account. Then, each pay period, you withdraw and distribute the budgeted amount into envelopes, one for each category of the Spending Plan—for example, giving, savings, mortgage, utilities, car payment. When it is time to make a purchase, you spend it out of the appropriate envelope. How much is there tells you how much you can spend.

> ## THREE SYSTEMS FOR KEEPING TRACK OF YOUR **MONEY**
>
> - Envelope system
> - Written record
> - Electronic platform

Envelope System: A tangible way to designate money for various expenses

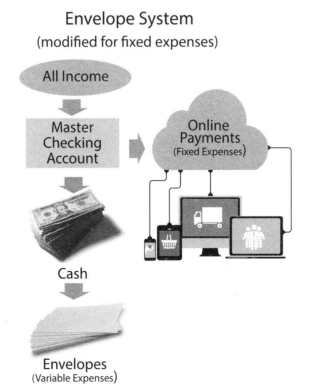

Envelope System

All Income

Master Checking Account

Cash

Envelopes

Envelope System
(modified for fixed expenses)

All Income

Master Checking Account

Online Payments
(Fixed Expenses)

Cash

Envelopes
(Variable Expenses)

Obviously, it wouldn't be practical or wise to have an envelope for every category on the Spending Plan form—take mortgage or rent as an example. You probably wouldn't want an envelope with that much cash sitting around. Not to mention, there are certain creditors who won't take cash. You can pay those categories by check or online from your bank account. The diagram on the right-hand side of the page reflects these types of payments. You still deposit all income into a master bank account. But you don't have envelopes for those categories for which you write monthly checks or have monthly withdrawals. This would include things like your mortgage, utilities, and car payment. Note that these expenses are often fixed monthly amounts and controlling them is not typically a problem. But for variable categories like food, clothing, entertainment, and household, which are more difficult to control, you have envelopes. When the money runs out of that envelope, you're done with those purchases for the month.

A big advantage of this system is that you don't have to keep any written records. The envelopes and your ledger (or online account or budgeting app) become your record-keeping system. You put the budgeted amounts into each envelope, and what's left at the end of the month tells you how much you spent.

Another huge advantage is that each time you go to an envelope to get cash is a tangible reminder of how much you have to spend. You thought you'd like to eat out for dinner but there's only $23 in the entertainment envelope. In that case, you have dinner at home and go out and enjoy the ambiance of your favorite restaurant for dessert and coffee. That consistent feedback provides a powerful check-and-balance system. Putting the system in place will reduce spending.

If you have never budgeted before, or if you have tried and didn't succeed, this system may be the best one for you. However, it's not just for beginners. Many who have tried other systems and have budgeted for many years prefer this system because of its simplicity, and because it works.

Written Record System

In session 2 we introduced you to our written record-keeping form, called the Spending Record. If you've been using this form to track your expenses, we hope it's given you some good insights about your spending and that it was helpful in balancing your plan.

You can use this form by printing it out and writing on it or by accessing the digital version, and there are many ways to simplify its use. Turn to the Spending Record Example on the next page. If you elect to use this system, each month you would enter your Spending Plan figures for each category on line #1. At the end of the month, after totaling your expenses, you would use line #3, (Over)/Under, to record the difference between what your plan called for and what was actually spent (the difference between lines #1 and #2). If you use the paper form, you will find it helpful to subtotal at least some of the categories at the end of each week to get a feel for what you've spent to that point. If you use the digital version of the form, the math is done for you.

Note that it's not necessarily bad if you overspend in a category in a given month. The Spending Plan form is set up to reflect averages. But, since most months are not average, some categories may be a little higher or lower than the budgeted amount. Spending more than the monthly allocated amount for clothing in January to get great after-holiday sales may be wise, but you'll need to have spent under the allocated amount in past months or spend less in future months to balance out. Be careful that this doesn't get to be a month-to-month rationale, "Oh, I'll spend less next month in that category!"

A couple of additional points about the use of the Spending Record Form. There are two optional rows at the bottom of the sheet—lines #4 and #5. These are year-to-date totals you can use to keep track of your progress through the year. It would let you see not only how you did that month, but also how you are doing so far that year. An explanation of how to arrive at those figures appears in your appendix on page 155, "Keeping Year-to-Date Totals on the Spending Record."

On the "monthly regular expenses" side of the Spending Record Example (page 115), there is a monthly assessment space where you can make notes regarding special circumstances (positive or negative) that occurred that month. Those notes can be very helpful six months later when you're trying to remember what happened that made that month so different.

Another hint to make written record keeping simpler is to take advantage of "even billing" (sometimes called "balanced billing") when possible. Check to see if you can make your insurance payments in equal monthly installments

SPENDING RECORD EXAMPLE

Daily Variable Expenses

	Transportation		Household						Professional Services	Entertainment		
	Gas, etc.	Maint./Repair	Groceries	Clothes	Gifts	Household Items	Personal	Other		Going Out	Travel	Other
(1) Spending Plan	200	40	480	150	80	75	50	---	---	100	70	40
	64	21	186	89	17	14	16	25		22	70	22 (sitter)
	42		22	46	55	22	18			46		
	38		20	50		9				19		
	85		172			31						
			81									
			8									
			20									
(2) Total	202	21	446	185	72	76	34	25	---	87	70	22
(3) (Over)/Under	(2)	19	34	(35)	8	(1)	16	(25)	---	13	---	18
(4) Last Mo. YTD												
(5) This Mo. YTD												

- Use this page to record expenses that tend to be daily, variable expenses—often the hardest to control.
- Keep receipts throughout the day and record them at the end of each day.
- Total each category at the end of the month (line 2) and compare to the Spending Plan (line 1). Subtracting line 2 from line 1 gives you an (over) or under the budget figure for that month (line 3).
- To verify that you have made each day's entry, cross out the number at the bottom of the page that corresponds to that day's date.
- Optional: If you wish to monitor your progress as you go through the year, you can keep cumulative totals in lines 4 and 5.

SPENDING RECORD EXAMPLE

MONTH: January

Monthly Regular Expenses (generally paid by check once a month)

	Giving		Savings	Debt			Housing				Auto Payments	Insurance		Misc. Cash Expenses
	Church	Other		Credit Cards	Education	Other	Mortgage/ Rent	Maintenance	Utilities	Other		Auto/ Home	Life/ Medical	
(1) Spending Plan	280	30	155	75	50	---	970	30	180	25	350	90	40	65
	140	20	155	75	50		970		95 (elec)	44	350	90	40	65
	140	10	200						31 (gas)					
									79 (tel)					
(2) Total	280	30	355	75	50	---	970	---	205	44	350	90	40	65
(3) (Over)/Under	---	---	(200)	---	---	---	---	30	(25)	(19)	---	---	---	---
(4) Last Mo. YTD														
(5) This Mo. YTD														

- This page allows you to record major monthly expenses for which you typically write just one or two checks per month.
- Entries can be recorded as the checks are written (preferably) or by referring back to the check ledger at a convenient time.
- Total each category at the end of the month (line 2) and compare to the Spending Plan (line 1). Subtracting line 2 from line 1 gives you an (over) or under the budget figure for that month (line 3).
- Use the "Monthly Assessment" section to reflect on the future actions that will be helpful in staying on course.

MONTHLY ASSESSMENT

Area	(Over)/Under	Reason	Future Action
Clothes	(35)	After-Christmas sales	No new clothes next month
Savings	(200)	Gift from Aunt May	N/A
Utilities	(25)	Electricity and phone	check phone plan
Insurance	90	Quarterly bill next month	N/A

Areas of Victory   *Feels great to be ahead on savings. Thanks, Aunt May! I'm really proud of how we're doing!*

Areas to Watch   *Need to look hard at ways to save on electricity and phone bills.*

and check with your utility companies to see if you qualify for their balanced billing system, which evens your payments out over the year and makes budgeting simpler.

Using Digital Resources

About now some of you are probably thinking, "Why are you messing around with envelopes and writing things down when there's great budgeting software out there that does it all? It adds and subtracts for you, does charts and graphs, prints out spreadsheets, maintains running balances and provides all kinds of helpful reports."

There's no question that there are software programs, online services, and apps out there that have wonderful features. If you do choose to use them, keep some things in mind. First, most of these programs will require you to invest some time up front to learn their program, to set up your accounts, and get connected with your bank. Most financial software programs have very thorough instruction and user guides. Make sure you have the time and the desire to learn all you need to in order to use them effectively.

Also, be aware that some of these programs default to simply tracking expenses. You'll need to make sure you're using the software or app functions that allow you to set spending targets and compare actual versus planned spending. Otherwise you aren't really budgeting.

There are a number of apps that can turn your smartphone into a budgeting tool. These allow you to record your transactions in real time, photograph and sort your receipts, and keep track of your budgeting goals all in one place. Take advantage of whatever technological resources appeal to you and make it easier to track your spending and reach your financial goals.

Activity: Selecting Your Record-Keeping System

1. Have you already been using one of the systems above that we've mentioned? If so, what do you like or dislike about it?

2. Select which record-keeping system you plan to use to implement your Spending Plan: envelope, written record, electronic, or a combination.

If you plan on using the written or digital systems, transfer the numbers from your Spending Plan form to the first lines of the blank Spending Record Form on pages 167–168 of your Appendix. You can use those numbers to help you set up your electronic record-keeping system.

> If you receive more than one paycheck per month, create a plan for which expenses will be paid out of each paycheck. For a sample plan, see page 159 in the Appendix.

If you plan on using the envelope system, use the Envelope Record-Keeping Worksheet, found on page 165 of the Appendix to designate your spending categories and amounts. Under the Checks/Automatic Withdrawal section, write in any expenses you plan to pay with a check or automatic withdrawal.

Dealing with Implementation Issues

We want to alert you to a couple of issues you may encounter as you begin implementing your Spending Plan and record-keeping system. One issue is how to allocate your money when you get paid more than once per month. The solution is to create a plan for which expenses will be paid out of each paycheck. While it may take a little time initially to set this up, it will eliminate all the questions, anxiety, and uncertainty about how each paycheck is allocated. A fuller explanation and an example of how to do this are on page 159 in your Appendix, "More Than One Paycheck per Month."

> If you have money accumulating in certain categories, transfer funds from those categories into a short-term savings account. Use a simple ledger to keep track of how much money in the account is in each category. For a sample ledger, see page 162 in the Appendix.

The second issue you might encounter is money accumulating in certain categories. While that may sound like a nice problem to have, in reality you may not want to have large amounts building up in certain envelopes or in your bank account. For example, if you take one big vacation a year, for eleven months before the trip, the money will pile up in your vacation envelope. That creates two concerns: one, you could be tempted to "borrow" the funds for other things; two, having a large amount of cash on hand could be a security risk. Similarly, if you use the written or digital record-keeping system, a balance would accumulate in your bank account, potentially giving the impression that you have extra money to spend.

To avoid these situations, we recommend money for these types of categories should be deposited each payday, preferably by direct deposit, into a short-term savings account (probably the same account used for emergency savings). The funds are then withdrawn when it's time to use them. If you're wondering, "How will I know how much money is for what purpose if I put all the money into just one account?" there is a simple form to keep track of that, and an explanation of the process is found on page 160 in your Appendix, "Money Building Up in Certain Categories."

Activity: Obstacles

You've read about a few of issues you may encounter when you begin implementing your Spending Plan and record-keeping system. For your particular situation, what are some other obstacles you might face?

My biggest obstacle(s):

Dealing with Emergencies

One of the biggest issues first-time budgeters face is failing to have emergency savings to draw on when the unexpected happens. For example, let's say you put aside $100 per month—$1,200 for the year—for auto repair. Let's say that amount is, in fact, exactly the amount you'll wind up spending over the course of the year. Unfortunately, the second month of your budgeting process rolls around and you get hit with a brake job that costs $400.

Here's what not to do in this situation: say, "I give up. This system doesn't work. I can't drive my car without brakes, and I can't get to work without a car. I only have $100 set aside from last month, and $100 budgeted this month so, clearly, I have to use my credit card to get the brakes fixed."

Avoid that temptation. You've made a commitment, and it includes incurring no new debt. So what is the alternative? First, look at every other area of your Spending Plan and look for any opportunity to cut back on expenses that month and apply those dollars to the brake job. If, after doing that, you still don't have enough, continue to think creatively.

"Okay, I can't drive the car without brakes, but do I really need a brake job right now? No, what I really need is a way to get back and forth to work. Does that mean I have to get the car repaired now? No, maybe that means I need to carpool, or ride a bus, or share our second car with my spouse or find some other way to get to work until we can save the money for the brake job." Maybe it means borrowing a car from a friend or letting your church know that you have a temporary need—there are lots of God's cars in every local church!

The point is, think creatively, make sacrifices when necessary, and stick to your commitment to incur no new debt! Pray and let others know of your need.

Our grandparents didn't always have credit cards. They had to be creative when something came up and they didn't have the money. Don't just cave and pull out your credit card at the first obstacle you face.

> **DEALING WITH EMERGENCIES**
> - Keep your commitment not to incur new debt.
> - Look at your Spending Plan to see where else you may be able to save money.
> - Think creatively.
> - Let others know of your need.

> The more we become financially faithful, the closer we get to true financial well-being.

Committing to the Process

We're near the end of the study, so let's take a few minutes to look back at what we've covered.

First, we became aware of the dilemma we face between following the pull of the consumer culture when it comes to finances or seeking the faithful way to financial well-being.

Foolish

Faithful

The Consumer
Culture

The Faithful
Way

We talked about the daily decisions we make that lead us to either foolishly follow cultural messages or faithfully move toward God. We also learned that when you faithfully move toward God, you increasingly become a:

Diligent Earner,

Generous Giver,

Wise Saver,

Cautious Debtor,

and Prudent Spender.

We have said that as we become those things, as we become financially faithful, we experience a growing sense of financial well-being.

Activity: My Vision for Becoming Financially Faithful, Financially Free

If you could become financially faithful and experience true financial well-being, what would your life be like? How do you think it would change your life?

My answer:

Activity: My Commitment Plan

You now have a vision for what can happen by following the principles in this study. In addition, you have a first draft of a Spending Plan in hand and a record-keeping system to track your progress.

Now, it's commitment time. We encourage you to complete the Commitment Plan below to remind you of why you wanted to do this in the first place and to refer back to when you face obstacles in following your plan.

The first statement on the Commitment Plan asks for a date by which you will begin implementing your Spending Plan and keeping records. Take a moment and fill in that date.

The next statement asks for the name of an accountability partner. Write down the name of someone who will be an encouragement and help hold you accountable to following your plan.

COMMITMENT PLAN

I will begin implementing my Spending Plan and keeping records by _____.

My accountability partner will be _____.

I will pray daily for God's help and encouragement.

Notice the last statement of your Commitment Plan, "I will pray daily for God's help and encouragement." We said at the beginning of the study that making some of the changes required to get our financial lives in order will take the power of the Holy Spirit to help us. Your daily prayers will open the door for the Spirit to work within you and help you stay the course.

Commit to using your Spending Plan and record-keeping system for at least ninety days. This will give you enough time to develop new habits and begin to see the first benefits of your efforts. Don't be discouraged after the first month. This initial data may only show whether the estimates on your Spending Plan worksheet are realistic. It could take three or four months to determine accurate figures for some of your categories. At that time, you can make adjustments to your plan. Some of the data you obtain may be good news. You may discover that your efforts have resulted in lower expenses than you initially projected.

KEEPING YOUR COMMITMENT TO THE SPENDING PLAN

- Commit to using your Spending Plan and record-keeping system for at least ninety days.
- Do not become discouraged after the first month—adjustments are normal.
- Seek assistance, if needed.

Adjustments are normal. One month is not definitive. You are looking for patterns that emerge over several months. Get assistance if needed. If a question arises and you don't know the answer, find someone who can help, like a financial counselor or a friend who is financially knowledgeable. Maybe your church has a ministry or a member who provides budget counseling.

There's hope for everyone, no matter what your situation. It's amazing to see how God works through our openness to prayer and spiritual reflection in our financial lives. A commitment to financial well-being puts us in the position to see God's love and provision. We realize what God has been doing all along as we become more attentive to the wonderful gifts we are given and help that is offered.

In the Book of Malachi, God speaks to the people and asks them to bring their offerings on the assumption that they are giving in an environment of abundance. "Please test me," God says. "See whether I do not open all the windows of the heavens for you and empty out a blessing until there is enough" (Malachi 3:10). What if we trusted that we will see blessings as we attend to our financial life?

God of abundant life, we know that in your power you work transformations in the world and in our lives. You change us from within and make each of us a new person. Help us to claim a new way of thinking and a new way of living and to be good stewards of what you've entrusted to us. Empower us to live humbly and walk with you. We yearn to hear your words, "Well done, good and faithful servant, good and faithful trustee"; in Christ's name we pray. Amen.

Activity: Wrapping Up

- What part of this study's teaching has really stuck with you?

- In what ways are you most encouraged to discover God's intentions for your flourishing through your finances?

Becoming a Financial Leader for Your Congregation

One of the consistent themes you have seen in this book is that our financial lives are part of our spiritual lives. One of the reasons Jesus talked so much about money is because he realized that our overall well-being is reflected in the ways we deal with (or don't deal with) our finances. Helping us tend to our attitudes toward money is part of the way he helps us tend to our souls.

CLERGY VIDEOS

Videos for the clergy sessions are available at AmplifyMedia.com (search Saving Grace) and are included on the *Saving Grace* DVD.

As clergypersons, we have a special responsibility to help those we serve face courageously this area of their lives in order to conquer the fears and worries that lurk there. To do that effectively, we first have to understand our own fears and worries. The work you have done in other areas of this book will help build your self-awareness as you approach this area of ministry with others.

Many of us came through our theological education without much training in being financial leaders in the church. In the process of receiving our education, we may have also collected some new financial worries of our own in the form of educational loans that need to be repaid (with the modest salary of an entry-level minister). We also may have grown up with messages from our family and churches, spoken and unspoken, that portrayed discussing money in church as distasteful at best and taboo at worst.

If any of these situations seem familiar, you'll understand why it's clear that we've got to reorient our own thinking. This book has presented you with a great method to start approaching your own financial health. Now we want to talk about how to become a financial leader in your congregation.

To do this we're going to explore and claim the Jesus attribute of boldness. Jesus was unafraid to confront powers that kept people from flourishing. The healing stories in the Gospels show Jesus telling off demons and challenging people unable to walk to take up their bed and do just that. He seemed to be able to see into the lives of people, whether a Samaritan woman at a well or a rich young man, and to know what was holding them back from the fullness of life God intended for them. But beyond that, Jesus was able to speak and act in bold ways that brought physical and spiritual healing to those who needed it.

Boldness is a disruptive quality. It refuses to let important things go unsaid, and it is discontented with the status quo. A Christian life oriented toward holiness harnesses courage to keep exploring every aspect of our lives and to offer them to God for transformation. The Letter to the Ephesians encourages Christians to do this kind of work. "Test everything to see what's pleasing to the Lord," the writer says. "Everything exposed to the light is revealed by the light. Everything that is revealed by the light is light. Therefore, it says, *Wake up, sleeper! Get up from the dead, and Christ will shine on you*" (Ephesians 5:10, 13-14).

As a clergyperson, you can help people bring their financial lives into the light and discover healing and hope for themselves and their loved ones. What a powerful ministry that would be!

Clergy as Financial Leaders

Most churches feel that they're in a financial crunch. Looking back on the golden years of the church's history, church leaders will recall (even if it wasn't quite so) that there was money enough and to spare for staff salaries, programming, missions, maintenance, and all of the other things that comprise a church budget. Today, some churches worry about how they'll even keep the doors open. Spending has been scaled back. Pastoral salaries are in decline. And the big givers of yesteryear have not been replaced.

What's a bold pastoral leader to do in such an environment? One well-worn preacher's story describes a pastor who stands in front of the congregation and declares, "The good news is that this church has all the money it needs. The hard news is that it's in your pockets." Such a story presumes that the abundance is there; the problem is that we just haven't given from it.

Operating from an assumption that God provides all we need to succeed in ministry is an important part of leading your congregation into financial health. But there is another, equally important part of this leadership. What your church also needs is a vision that is compelling, faithful, and God-sized.

In her book *Dream Like Jesus: Deepen Your Faith and Bring the Impossible to Life*, United Methodist leader Rebekah Simon-Peter asks, "What if the problem isn't the people in the pews—rural or urban—but the way spiritual leaders lead them?" What many churches lack, and what leads them into decline, Simon-Peter says, is "a bold vision, a vision that reflects Jesus' dream of heaven on earth" (Knoxville, TN: Market Square Books, 2019; 30).

Spiritual leaders get the connection between the vision and the funding. Money problems are not ultimately resource problems; they're matters of faith reflecting our most fundamental beliefs about God and what God can do. If we hear Jesus say that "whoever believes in me will do the works that I do. They will do even greater works than these" (John 14:12), it should make us think twice about saying, "I can't."

As clergy leaders, entrusted with proclaiming the good news of Jesus, we ought to feel at home in the vision business. After all, the gospel message is all about transformation—transformed lives and a transformed world. Perhaps it's some relief to know that we don't have to move away from that familiar terrain when we think about financial leadership. What we do have to do is see money as one of those things that God uses to transform.

John Wesley used to send his preachers out with the admonition that they had "nothing else to do except save souls." That's another way of saying that we want to see the powerful effect of God's saving action in the lives of those we serve. When you help people live into a God-sized dream and help them see how they can use every resource available, including their money, to bring it to life, you are doing saving work.

Simon-Peter's book is a good resource for helping claim this area of pastoral leadership. Other resources, like Kim Klein's *Ask and You Shall Receive* (Jossey-Bass, 2000) and J. Clif Christopher's *God vs. Money* (Abingdon, 2018), also help make this connection. And Tom Berlin's *The Generous Church: A Guide for Pastors* (Abingdon, 2016) contains great insight into what financial leadership means for pastors and practical advice on how to approach it with a clear and effective strategy.

Preaching and Teaching About Money

Thinking about preaching as a tool for helping congregations shift their attitudes and culture regarding finances is only one part of financial leadership. If we reduce communication about finances solely to an annual sermon (which most people will avoid if they know it's coming), we lose the opportunity to do the kind of transformative work that will engage others in the process and relieve the stress we might feel about carrying the load for the whole congregation.

One resource that is particularly helpful in offering a broader perspective on how to develop a more holistic culture shift is *Church Finances for Missional Leaders: Best Practices for Faithful Stewardship* by Bonnie Ives Marden (Wesley's Foundery Books, 2019). While the book is designed for both lay and clergy leaders, one appendix deals particularly with the pastoral stewardship of giving and the ways pastors can move their congregations to healthier practices.

Marden emphasizes building literacy and familiarity with basic financial practices, something that is important for every clergyperson. Clergy should know what their church is doing in financial planning and management and know the people who are responsible for that, conferring with them regularly. Build relationships with your financial leadership so that you can guide them toward better practices.

Preaching is still one of the most visible and important means that pastors have for communicating with their congregations. And most clergypersons, even those who do not preach regularly, are involved in teaching the congregation in some way, whether that is a Sunday school class or Bible study, confirmation, or some other opportunity. Here are some ways you can make your preaching and teaching about money more effective:

Know your own story. All of us have histories with money. What's yours? Spend some time reflecting on the messages you grew up with regarding money. Did your family of origin have an ethic of abundance or scarcity? How did they handle times of financial stress? What financial stresses are you experiencing now? What steps are you taking to address them? Answering these questions can give you confidence and help you speak as a fellow-traveler with those you are addressing. Nothing is more powerful than the testimony of people who can share their authentic experiences of struggle and faith. This book also gives you the tools you need to begin your journey to greater financial freedom.

Preach and teach about money often, highlighting money-related themes in Scripture. It's not hard to find references to wealth, poverty, stewardship, money, and finances in the Bible. You will also see passages concerning generosity, trust, and abundant life. Seek out opportunities to lift up these themes and connect them to faithful living. Connect your offering time in worship with the sermon, highlighting the act of offering as a response to the particular word of the biblical text that you are using. Melvin and James Amerson's *Celebrating the Offering* (Discipleship Resources, 2008) offers inspiring and creative ideas for making that connection.

Use multiple ways of talking about giving. Some people will respond to messages that talk about giving as a way to step out in faith on a grand adventure. Others will need to hear about how their giving can extend the legacy of a church for future generations. Still others will want to know how their giving helps connect the church with the community and those in need. Some will jump on the bandwagon to be part of a churchwide campaign that unites the body of Christ. There are even some who will be motivated by the fact that there is a budget shortfall and they can help make a difference in closing the gap.

Invite some of your givers to offer testimonies in worship about their giving. Notice what they say about why they give. Meet with these volunteers before the service to help them craft their testimonies based on what you hear in their stories, guiding them to speak confidently in a way that will resonate with the congregation. They will give you clues about the many different motivations people bring to their giving. Helping people make the connection between those core motivations, their money, and their faith will enable you to be a more effective communicator in both your teaching and your preaching.

End with an ask. We've all been subjected to "may we" sermons. We've probably given more than a few ourselves. A "may we" sermon draws to a close with a gentle nudge to more reflection on the sermon's message. As in: "May we consider how God might use our gifts for the upbuilding of the kingdom." May we? Of course, we can! Let's do it. And let's give our listeners concrete ways to do it. Have you been talking about Jesus's concern for children and there's an elementary school down the street? What is something your congregation could do this week to make a difference for the children who attend there? How can the children in your church use their gifts in mission? Let's fund their dreams to serve God. Be bold and specific in your ask, and watch God work with it.

Connect your giving to your vision. As we've discussed above, people don't give to budgets; they give to God. If your church's vision isn't compelling enough to inspire people to give, maybe it's not big enough. Keeping the church's doors open is not a big vision. It's all that's left when all the other vision has left the building.

When preaching about money gets down to *shoulds* and *oughts*, it's a good sign that it's time to reorient around a different vision that is more faithful to the mission of the church for which Christ died. Sure, we should give, but what is the place in our soul that calls us to that practice? Sure, we ought to, but why? Make sure that you can answer those questions yourself before you ask anyone else to do so.

Stewardship and Financial Literacy Education

If you are finding this book helpful for growing in your own sense of financial well-being, think about how powerful it would be for others. Money and money management lead to deep spiritual struggles within individuals. Opening up to explore those struggles exposes a lot of vulnerable feelings. And addressing our financial concerns in the context of our faith can lead to huge transformations. Walking with people on this profound journey is a great pastoral privilege.

In this book we have talked about the difference between stewardship and ownership. Christians begin with a belief that "all things were created through [Christ] and for him" (Colossians 1:16). If God is the source of all things and all things find their end in God, then our role is to steward God's good gifts for God's glory and the benefit of God's creatures and creation.

A church's stewardship committee can highlight this theological perspective through its work. Unlike a finance committee, which may orient toward conserving funds and preparing for a rainy day, a good stewardship committee can take the lead in helping persons embrace God's abundance and discover the joy of generosity. While the stewardship committee may talk about the budget plans of the church and the challenges in meeting that budget, it will usually do so by inspiring the church members to see the gifts that surround them. Clergy should be a part of that stewardship team, creating the conversations that help people dive deeper into their beliefs about money and God's provision.

One part of this stewardship education could be a course on financial literacy to help persons grow in an area of life that they may have found uncomfortable to talk about. As individuals find more freedom in their own lives, they will have stories to share with others as they move your church toward more financial freedom.

Another area where stewardship teams can take the lead is in the promotion of designated giving. As part of a church's overall mission and vision, developing a cadre of persons who can present that mission to individuals in compelling ways to encourage giving to capital campaigns and other priorities in the church's work is transformative. Pastors should be part of that group, taking the lead in developing that message and presenting it to potential donors. Many United Methodist conferences have Foundations affiliated with them that offer excellent resources to help in this development.

Estate Planning

In the previous clergy section, we discussed personal estate planning. One part of the work of a stewardship committee is to establish educational opportunities on estate planning for church members. Individuals who set up planned giving have blessed many missions and ministries long after the time of their deaths. Churches that receive funds through planned giving need to have good policies and procedures in place to manage these gifts.

Talking with church members about how to use their accumulated wealth at the end of their lives might seem like a difficult conversation, but many people find it very rewarding to think about how their resources, however meager, can go on doing good for the causes and ministries they care about. Stewardship committees can open up these conversations through workshops on planned giving and estate planning. This sometimes opens the door to more pastoral conversations with the clergyperson. Clergy who have some knowledge about planned giving instruments can help advise, in these more personal settings, about how to connect donor values with ways to express those values. Having done the work on your own estate planning will enrich these conversations as well.

Planned giving can come in many forms. Donors may choose to make a bequest of cash, stocks, or property. Those gifts may also come in the form of charitable gift annuities or trusts. As a clergyperson, you should always direct donors to seek the advice of an attorney and financial planner to help them sort out the tax implications and correct instruments for their desired mode of giving. These instruments can be complex and require the help of professionals.

Endowments are funds that are restricted in use to allow for their continuation into the future. In general, the amount of the original gift, known as the principal, remains unspent in the fund unless the bequest's language or a policy allows for its use. The principal is invested so that it can produce interest or dividends that can be used for present purposes. Bequests often specify the uses to which the funds can be put.

United Methodist clergy have many estate planning resources available to them through Wespath Benefits and Investments (see the Clergy Appendix for a further description of these resources). In addition, the United Methodist Foundations have resources to help begin these discussions on a congregational level.

Conclusion

We've now reached the end of this book, but it's really the beginning. The test of this book's usefulness is how it impacts your behavior in the future. More than this, have you developed the eyes to see that the journey to financial freedom is part of the journey to greater holiness and abundant living? Jesus calls each of us into a transformed life, and God's intent is for you to experience that transformation in every aspect of your being.

If you are a clergyperson, your own transformation will be a blessing for those you serve as well. Like the aroma of the perfume that Mary poured over Jesus's feet as he sat at the table, the blessing you receive from giving concentrated attention to your finances will spread to others (John 12:3). You will have what you need to be a bold leader in your congregation.

Finally, a word about community. You are not in this alone. This book was created with the wisdom of a number of people and organizations who have been thinking for a long time about how to help clergy like you make the most of the resources they have been given. They have given you tools to help you get started.

Now you get to build your own team. Seek out the partners who will help you lead your congregation. Find a covenant community, perhaps of other pastors, who can help you set and keep goals in your spiritual journey, including financial goals. And don't be afraid to enlist professionals to help you with the many aspects of this journey. With a team, you will be stronger.

As Paul said to the Colossian Christians, "[May you] be filled with the knowledge of God's will, with all wisdom and spiritual understanding. We're praying this so that you can live lives worthy of the Lord and pleasing to him in every way: by producing fruit in every good work and growing in the knowledge of God; by being strengthened through [God's] glorious might so that you endure everything and have patience" (Colossians 1:9-11). Amen!

Discussion Questions

- Why is it important for pastors to be financial leaders in their congregations?

- Who else brings financial leadership to local churches, and how can pastors work together with them to lead faithfully and effectively?

- How do you currently approach preaching about money? What might you do differently as a result of completing this study?

- What stands out as especially challenging when it comes to being a financial leader in your congregation? How can improving your own financial literacy help in this regard?

- What do you see as the greatest need within your congregation regarding money?

- What do individual Christians and congregations stand to gain by achieving financial freedom? How do the goals of this program align with God's intentions for our flourishing?

Saving Grace in a Time of Crisis

In 2020, the economic shutdown due to the COVID-19 crisis put many people into a situation of financial crisis. Depending on the amount of savings you start with at the beginning of severe economic uncertainty, be prepared to revisit everything: spending, saving, investing in your retirement, your budget, your charitable giving.

Ask yourself, "What's really important?"

- When budgeting from a known set of income and expense assumptions, it's easy to project what you think is important into your financial planning.
- When job losses occur amidst otherwise normal economic times, you're on your own with thinking through your financial options.
- When the economy comes to a halt for everyone, there's no better time to reassess how you allocate your resources: your time, your emotional capacity, and your financial resources.

Cash is king

- If you're facing loss of income or concerned that might happen and you have limited savings, preserve your cash.

- Your banker or lender is your friend. Work with your bank, student loan servicer, or credit card company to defer or limit payments.

- Reduce, or if you must, suspend retirement savings—only until your financial situation stabilizes. Borrow from your retirement savings only as a last resort.

- Forget your budget, if you work from one—review every purchase for whether you need it, not whether you want it. Plan your spending week by week and make sure you can cover obligations that come due monthly.

Learn from your habits

- Sometimes what's happening around you will force you to change habits. During COVID-19 quarantining, how much less did you spend on transportation? dining out? coffee shops? non-food purchases? How much more did you spend on takeout? groceries?

- US retail sales fell a record 16 percent in the month of April 2020, the peak of a national lock-down (https://apnews. com/e95a6d2d0a721 fcffb4efb9435b84f4f).

Refinance debt if you can

- Lower interest rates are common during times of economic distress: take advantage of them if you can.

- If you are disciplined about not accumulating more credit card debt but have some you're working to pay off, perhaps you can eliminate your credit card debt with a modest cash-out mortgage refinancing and still lower your monthly interest rate.

- Though not ideal by any means and depending on your cash reserve level, you might need to consider lengthening the term of your mortgage. When things improve you can pay it off more quickly.

Learn from the past

Apply what you learned from the last economic hardship you lived through.

- What did you learn that you still apply today?
- What did you wish you knew then that you know now?
- What changes did you make in how you handled your finances that worked for you?
- What do you wish you had done differently?

Take advantage of government assistance

- To keep the economy going, the federal government sometimes fills the gap. During the COVID-19 pandemic, direct payments to individuals below certain income levels were made and unemployment insurance was enhanced. Employers were encouraged to retain employees rather than laying off through the Paycheck Protection Program (PPP).
- Policymakers take these actions with the hope that those eligible will avail themselves of the resources available.

Don't stop giving

- Generosity abounds in times of economic turmoil and distress. Sometimes it's from people who are blessed with resources, sometimes it's from people who have reprioritized what's most important, and sometimes it's reflected in non-monetary generosity.
- There are many ways to be generous without giving money:
  - Volunteer your time.
  - Volunteer your expertise (for example, during the COVID-19 crisis, many made face masks to help limit the spread of the virus).
  - Volunteer your social capital.

- Visit with those less fortunate and more isolated than you (and there will be many who are).
- Every little bit makes a difference
- Consider an automatic withdrawal, even a small amount, so the habit is nearly invisible

Options of last resort

- Borrowing from your retirement savings
- Missing mortgage or auto loan payments and putting your home in foreclosure or auto subject to repossession

When it's over (at least for you)

- Return to annual budgeting.
- Get back to your long-term plan as soon as you can.
- Replenish your cash reserves.
- Reduce your debt.
- Restore saving for your retirement.
- Increase your retirement savings rate.
- Give more.

APPENDIX

Contents

Earning

Determining an Average Month for Variable Income

The key to determining a budget in the case of a variable income (due to sales commissions or being self-employed, for example) is to make a conservative estimate of net income for the coming year. Where possible, this would be done on the basis of the past several years' income. Conservative means not allowing one really good year unduly influence the estimate for the coming year.

For example, if the past three years' net income were $37,000, $40,000, and $54,000, a conservative estimate for the coming year might be in the range of $44,000, not $56,000. The assumption is that this year may not be the exceptionally good year last year was. In this example, a monthly budget would be $44,000 divided by 12 or $3,667. In the months when income exceeds $3,667, the excess would be put in a short-term savings account to be drawn on in months when income is less than $3,667.

A wise approach to variable income also includes predetermining the best use of any additional funds, in the event actual income exceeds estimated income for the year. Thoughtful consideration before the fact will prevent impulsive decisions if and when the money becomes available, avoiding regrets afterward that it had not been used in some other, better way.

What Happens to Your Raises?

Most of the time, the extra money we earn in raises just gets used up. A few months later, we're not quite sure where it went. Yet, even a modest raise on a modest salary can add up to a significant amount of additional income in just a few years.

A 4% Annual Raise on a $30,000 Salary

	Year 1	Year 2	Year 3
4% raise	$31,200	$32,448	$33,745
Base Salary	$30,000	$30,000	$30,000
Additional Income	$1,200	$2,448	$3,745
Total additional income in three years = $7,393			

Consider the example in the chart above: a $30,000 salary and a 4 percent raise over a three-year period.

- The first year there is a $1,200 increase (4 percent of $30,000).
- The second-year salary is then $32,448, an additional margin of $2,448 from the original salary of $30,000.
- The third-year salary increases to $33,745, producing an increase from the original $30,000 of $3,745.

The total additional income in that three-year period adds up to almost $7,400—nearly one-fourth of the original salary. And that's just a three-year period! Taxes obviously impact the amount, but even the after-tax amount accumulates to a significant figure.

Deciding ahead of time how to use raises can be a key part of the strategy for reaching your financial goals.

Giving

Giving Assets upon One's Death

For many, planning your estate is the largest single act of financial stewardship you will ever make because you are giving from the largest portion of what you have. For most people a large majority of their net worth involves the equity in their home, life insurance, and various retirement funds.

A will or trust enables you to provide guardianship for minor children, trusteeship over life insurance proceeds and other assets, and in the process:

- Bless your heirs.

- Minimize or even eliminate taxes and fees.

- Impact your church or other charities you care about.

We recommend a three-step process as you consider a will or trust planning.

1. What do I have?

   Begin with home equity and stocks, bonds, and other investments. Be sure to include assets such as life insurance, a death benefit, an IRA, or a 401(k). There's no need to get an exact value on your stocks or IRA as they fluctuate on a daily basis. It is more important to use an intelligent estimate and to get a will in place as soon as possible. In most cases, you can revise and refine the details of your will or trust at a future date.

2. Inheritance

   A helpful guideline for inheritance is to give based on dependency and love. An inheritance will, of course, start with minor children. For young families, much of the inheritance may come from life insurance proceeds. Many insurance professionals suggest ten times your annual income in life insurance as a rule. This may change as your asset base grows over your lifetime.

As children become adults your inheritance goals may change based on their needs and maturity.

A common mistake people make is to think of wills and trusts as permanent decisions. Rather, create a will or trust based on your desired outcome should you die in the next three to five years. At the end of that time, meet with your professionals and take a fresh look based on your current situation and the laws at that time.

3. Stewardship

Distribution of our assets upon death includes providing for our minor children or dependent parents, for example, but it can also include giving to your local church or other charities. Often this can be done in ways that take advantage of existing tax laws and result in significant charitable giving with only fractional decrease in what is available to heirs.

There are many distribution options to be considered, such as:

1. A percentage of your assets to go to ministries. This could be 10 or 20 percent, or more.

2. An equal portion of your estate to charity and to children. For example, if you have three children, you might divide your estate into four equal parts with one fourth designated to charity.

3. Capping your children's inheritance with a certain amount going to each child and the balance going to charity.

It has been estimated that less than 30 percent of Americans have a current will (of course, a much higher percentage of Americans will eventually die). Careful planning for the distribution of assets upon our death is the final and perhaps the greatest act of stewardship most of us will have the opportunity to fulfill.

Saving

The Cumulative Effect of Little Things over an Extended Period

A faucet dripping once every second can add up to fifty gallons in one week. In the same way, a slow trickle of money can gradually fill financial reservoirs to overflowing or drain them dry. To have the financial well-being God intends, we need to learn how to use—rather than be victimized by—the cumulative effect of little things over an extended period.

Just a Dollar a Day

The cumulative effect of a little money, just one dollar a day, can be tremendous over a forty-five-year career depending on whether it is saved or added to debt. The chart on the next page compares saving the dollar in a piggy bank, or a tax-sheltered mutual fund with a 10 percent return, versus charging the dollar to a credit card and incurring a 20 percent interest charge.

Years	Piggy bank	Invested in a mutual fund with a 10 percent rate of return	Charged to a credit card with a 20 percent interest rate
5	$1,825	$2,329	−$2,957
10	$3,650	$6,080	−$10,316
15	$5,475	$12,121	−$28,626
20	$7,300	$21,849	−$74,190
25	$9,125	$38,751	−$187,566
30	$10,950	$62,752	−$469,681
35	$12,775	$103,391	−$1,171,674
40	$14,600	$168,842	−$2,918,457
45	$16,425	$274,250	−$7,265,012

Major Purchases

The cumulative effect has a great impact on every major purchase. A $20,000 item can cost as little as $17,700 or as much as $25,500 depending on whether we allow the cumulative effect to work for us by saving for it in advance, or against us by incurring debt to purchase now.

Consider this example:

To accumulate $20,000 in five years at 5 percent interest, monthly payments to ourselves will have to be $295, and the total of the sixty payments will be $17,700.

To borrow $20,000 for five years at 10 percent interest, monthly payments to the finance company will have to be $425, and the total of the sixty payments will be $25,500.

Start Young

Although students and young adults may not feel they have much in the way of assets, the greatest asset they have is time.

PERSON A—EARLY START

Saving $100 a month during the first 15 years of a career, and then saving nothing more for the next 25 years with a 10 percent return, results in savings of $431,702.

PERSON B—LATE START

Saving nothing during the first 15 years of a career, and then saving $100 a month for the next 25 years with a 10 percent return, results in savings of $123,332.

Note: Person A contributed $18,000; Person B contributed $30,000

Life Expectancy and Replacement Costs of Various Household Items

As can be seen below, both the life expectancy and the cost of household items can vary widely. The use of resources like *Consumer Reports* can be helpful in determining the best balance between cost and quality on many items.

Item	Life Expectancy	Cost to Replace
Appliances		
Dishwasher	7–10 years	$350–$2,000
Dryer	15 years	$500–$2,000
Garbage disposal	8–15 years	$100–$300
Microwave oven	7–9 years	$100–$750
Oven/range	15–20 years	$300–$2,000
Refrigerator	13–15 years	$500–$4,000
Washing machine	10–15 years	$500–$2,000
Cooling		
Central air	10–15 years	$3,000–$7,000
Heat pump	12–15 years	$3,000–$8,000
Window AC unit	10 years	$150–$500
Heating		
Forced air furnace	10–20 years	$2,500–$6,000
Plumbing		
Hot water heater	5–15 years	$450–$2,000
Septic/sewer pump	5–7 years	$1,000–$2,000
Well pump	15 years	$1,000–$2,000

Item	Life Expectancy	Cost to Replace
Appliances		
Well pump	15 years	$1,000–$2,000
Roof Covering		
Asphalt standard shingle	20 years	$3–$4/sq. foot
Asphalt premium shingle	25 years	$4–$6/sq. foot
Wood shingle	30 years	$5–$9/sq. foot
Clay tile	40–50 years	$15–$20/sq. foot
Slate tile	40–80 years	$30–$50/sq. foot
Roll roofing	8–10 years	$3–$5/sq. foot

The Downside of Taking Loans from Retirement Accounts

The ability to take loans and make "hardship" withdrawals from a company-sponsored retirement plan, such as a 401(k) or 403(b) plan, makes the money in such plans a tempting source of cash. In addition to violating the basic principle that these funds have been set aside for the long-term future, there are significant downsides to borrowing from them.

Borrowing money from your 401(k) or 403(b) plan is allowable by law, but not by every employer. If your employer offers this feature, it usually comes with some limits. For example, you may not be able to borrow more than 50 percent of your vested account balance (that is, the portion of the employer contribution that belongs to you; this typically increases to 100 percent, or "fully vested," over a period of time) and only up to a maximum amount—often $50,000.

Disadvantages of borrowing from your retirement plan include:

- Money borrowed from a plan must be repaid with interest.

- Borrowing against your retirement plan reduces the amount that could be earning tax-deferred investment returns for your future.

- Repayment must be made within five years. Failure to do so incurs tax and penalty costs. An exception is money borrowed for the purchase of a home, in which case repayment may be extended to ten or fifteen years.

- You'll end up being taxed twice on the money you use to repay your loan, first because money you use to repay the loan is after-tax money, and second because you'll be taxed on the money when you withdraw it in retirement.

- If you leave your employer, you'll need to quickly repay the full amount of your loan—often within sixty days. Otherwise, the loan amount will be considered an early distribution, in which case you will owe taxes and an early withdrawal penalty.

- Under certain circumstances, such as difficulty paying medical bills or your mortgage, you may qualify for a hardship withdrawal from a 401(k) or 403(b) plan. In such cases, the money does not have to be repaid. However, taxes are due along with a 10 percent penalty—a heavy price to pay in addition to potentially not being prepared for retirement.

Debt

Establishing a Debt Repayment Plan

1. Establish a Spending Plan based on a temporary, spartan lifestyle.

   This frees up every possible dollar for the top priority of debt reduction and establishing an emergency fund.

2. Determine whether any nonessential assets can be sold.

   Cash from the sale of assets can be used to give the debt repayment process a kick-start and provide an initial savings buffer to ensure success.

3. List your debts from smallest to largest.

   Do not pay attention to the interest rate of the debt.

4. Pay the current minimum payment on all debts and the maximum additional possible on the smallest.

   Continue paying the current minimum payments, even if the credit card company lowers the required minimum payment as the principal is reduced. The goal is to pay off smaller debts quickly. This will give a sense of accomplishment as well as simplify the process as the number of creditors is reduced. Although one could argue that the greatest overall savings would occur by paying off the highest interest debt first, the psychological impact of getting some debts paid quickly far exceeds the downside of the few additional interest dollars it may cost. When only debts of relatively the same amount remain to be paid, apply extra payment to the one with the highest interest.

5. As each debt is paid off, add the total amount you were paying to the next largest debt.

    Add that amount to the minimum payment you were making.

6. Continue this strategy until all debts are paid.

    Do not reduce the total amount going to debt repayment as some debts are paid off. This creates a cumulative effect of adding the previous payment into the next largest debt that gives this system its power.

7. Incur no new debt.

    Discipline will be necessary in this regard. Obviously, you will not make progress if you are continuing to incur new debt as you are attempting to pay off the old. Be creative. Have someone hold you accountable. Ask for God's help. Know in your heart you are doing the right thing.

8. Discard credit cards.

    Get rid of them. If you must have a card for travel or emergency, have only one.

9. Reward yourself occasionally but modestly.

    As progress is made and milestones are reached, it is appropriate to reward yourself. For some, the progress itself may be reward enough. The following page shows a sample Debt Reduction Plan and an explanation for each column. A blank Debt Reduction Plan is included in the Forms section on page 163.

How Extra Payments Can Dramatically Reduce Your Mortgage Debt

Making even modest additional payments to your mortgage can have a significant impact on your pay-off date and the amount of interest you pay.

SAMPLE DEBT REDUCTION PLAN

Item	Amount Owed	Interest	Minimum Monthly Payment	Additional Payment	Payment Plan and Pay-off Dates					
				$ 150	3 Months	6 Months	15 Months	22 Months	26 Months	
Target	#372	18.0	$15	$165	Paid!					
Doctor	$550	0	$20	$20	$185	Paid!				
Visa	$1980	19.0	$40	$40	$40	$225	Paid!			
MasterCard	$2369	16.9	$50	$50	$50	$50	$275	Paid!		
Auto	$7200	6.9	$259	$259	$259	$259	$259	$259	Paid!	
Total	$12,471		$384	$534	$534	$534	$534	$534	$534	0

- The first and second columns list to whom the debt is owed and the amount owed. Debts are listed in the order of lowest to highest amount.
- The third and fourth columns list the interest rate and the minimum monthly payment for each debt.
- The fifth column indicates the amount of additional payment above the minimum that can be made and adds that amount to the minimum payment for the first (smallest) debt listed.
- The remaining columns show how, as each debt is paid, the payment for it is rolled down to the next debt. Pay-off dates can be calculated in advance or simply recorded as they are achieved.

The chart below is based on a $200,000 thirty-year mortgage at a 7 percent fixed interest rate. The monthly payments for this loan would be $1,331*. At $100 extra per month, which is just under one extra payment per year, the mortgage would be paid off in twenty-four years with a savings of more than $63,000 in interest.

Extra Payment	Out of Debt in . . .	Total Interest Paid	Interest Saved
$0/month	30 years	$279,022	—
$25/month	28 years	$259,278	$19,744
$50/month	27 years	$242,589	$36,433
$100/month	24 years	$215,709	$63,313

* $1,331 is just for the principal and interest on the loan. Monthly payments usually include an additional amount for taxes and homeowner's insurance, as well as private mortgage insurance if there is not a significant down payment.

Understanding Your Credit Score

What is a credit score? The credit score is the number on a person's credit report that tells a creditor whether that person is a dependable, reliable customer and credit risk. The score is formulated based on a person's financial history. It gives creditors an indication of how well that person manages his or her finances. It ranges from 300 to 850, and the higher the range, the better your credit score. For example: 300-629 is a negative score, 630-689 is average, 690-719 is good, and 720-850 is an excellent score.

There are six indicators that drive this number, and each reflects a percentage of your credit score: your payment history (35 percent), your credit utilization ratio (30 percent), the length of your credit history (15 percent), types of credit used (10 percent), and the number of hard credit inquiries (10 percent).

Your payment history shows how well you have managed your credit cards and loans, whether you paid them on time, and whether you missed payments. The credit utilization ratio is the total amount of credit you have used divided by your credit limit. For example, if you have a credit card with a credit limit of $5,000 and you have used $2,500 of that of that limit, the utilization ratio would be 40 percent. The length of your credit history is how long you have had your oldest account and the average time you have had your combined accounts. The longer you have had an account open, the greater the positive impact on your credit score.

The type of credit used also makes a difference to your credit report. It is good to have a mixture of revolving debt (credit cards) and installment debt (loans). Finally, hard credit inquiries are when creditors request your credit report, specifically, when you are applying for a credit card or an installment loan. A high number of hard inquiries shows that you are often seeking credit and may reflect negatively on your credit score. Paying off loans, keeping credit card balances low, paying all bills on time, and infrequently applying for credit all work together toward an excellent credit score.

You can obtain your credit score for free once a year from any of the credit reporting agencies: Experian, Equifax, or TransUnion. Many credit card companies also offer an online report of your credit score as a service along with your account.

Spending

Resisting the Urge to Purchase

Understanding the forces at work and your particular motivation for buying can be helpful in overcoming the urge to purchase. Is your trip to your favorite store or website the result of a spat with your spouse or a particularly large number when you stepped on the scale? Did you just get a raise and feel you absolutely deserve to spend some of it right now? Or, were you feeling lonely and are just so grateful to the solicitous salesperson who seemed to be the first person in a very long time to care about what might make you happy? (Remember, that may be true but it's also part of the salesperson's job.)

Psychologist April Benson, author of *I Shop, Therefore I Am*, gives all her clients a laminated card with six questions on it to put in their wallet on top of their credit cards. She suggests pausing every time you approach the register and asking yourself:

- Why am I here?
- How do I feel?
- Do I need this?
- What if I wait?
- How will I pay for it?
- Where will I put it?

Another helpful approach is to make the commitment to wait thirty days before purchasing that new thing you would like to have. Write it down on a card with the date. If within the thirty-day waiting period you find something else you want more than the original thing, write it down, scratch out the original, and begin a new thirty-day waiting period. Many have found that in following this process they seldom get to the end of thirty days with a given item. If they do, the above six questions can then be employed as a further check as to the advisability of the purchase.

A Big Difference in a Short Time: Buying a Used Car

Except for housing (an expense that may be hard to change), cars are the biggest drain on most budgets. The average price of a new car in the United States in 2020 is around $37,000. Although cars remain reliable for an average of over thirteen years and 145,000 miles, Americans tend to keep cars an average of only four years and 55,000 miles. Hanging on to your present car—or buying a good used car instead of a new one—may be the "one big thing" you could do to free up a significant amount of money for higher purposes.

Here are some facts you might consider when you decide whether having an older car is appropriate for you:

- A car loses most of its trade-in value in the first four years. If you trade in a new car after four or fewer years, you're paying a tremendous price for less than one-third the useful life of the car. On the other hand, if you buy a good used vehicle, you can get more than two-thirds of the useful life of the car at a relatively thrifty price.

- We typically assume that new cars are more reliable than used cars. However, according to *Consumer Reports*, cars less than one year old make as many trips to the repair shop as cars that are four or five years old. The most reliable years of a car's life are the second and third years.

- When you select a new car, you have to base your decision on the manufacturer's claims, but used cars have a track record you can check. Most libraries have the annual buying guide published by *Consumer Reports*, which rates used cars and provides repair records for most models. Information is also available on www.consumer

reports.org. Also, you can visit the National Highway Traffic Safety Administration website (www.nhtsa.gov) or call (800-424-9153) to check if a used car has ever been recalled.

- As a car gets older, the costs for gas and oil increase, but the costs for collision and theft insurance decrease.

- New car dealers typically save the best trade-in cars to sell on their own used car lots. These cars are often thoroughly checked and backed by a used car warranty. In some cases, used car buyers may even inherit the remainder of the manufacturer's new car warranty.

- Recently, leasing has become a popular option and is pushed heavily by many auto dealers. No wonder—it's a good deal for them. The appeal to many customers is the lower monthly payment. While at the end of a lease you don't own the car, many choose to enter a lease in order to always have a reliable car at a low payment. The upside for used car buyers is that an increasing number of leased cars are being turned in at the end of the lease and then turn up on used car lots.

Bottom Line:

- A comparison of the cost differential of keeping a four-year-old car for another four years and spending more on gas, oil, tires, and maintenance versus buying a new car showed the savings in keeping the four-year-old car to be over $6,000, assuming the new car would be paid for in cash. Add a couple thousand more dollars if it would be financed.

- A comparison of buying a two-year-old used car and keeping it for eight years versus leasing a new car every three years over a "driving lifetime" of forty-eight years revealed a staggering (almost unbelievable) differential of over $400,000.

How to Get the Most Out of Every Tank of Gas

- Observe the speed limit.
- Take heavy objects out of your trunk.

- While waiting for a train, or any similar wait of more than a minute or two, turn off the engine.
- Keep your tires properly inflated.
- Keep your engine properly tuned.
- Change air filters regularly.
- Accelerate slowly and smoothly.
- Combine trips.
- Find someone to share the ride.
- Consider fuel economy when choosing your next vehicle.

Source: www.fueleconomy.gov

To Buy or Not to Buy: Deciding to Rent or Purchase a Home

If you rent an apartment you've probably been told that you're throwing money away, that real estate is the best investment you can make, and other bits of conventional wisdom. But home ownership is not necessarily best for everyone. Here are some factors to consider.

How Much Can You Put Down?

Low- and no-down payment mortgages became popular in recent years and helped drive up the percentage of households that own their own home. They also drove up the number of foreclosures.

It is best to wait to buy until you can afford to make a 20 percent down payment. With such a down payment you will have proven you are disciplined at saving and you will avoid having to pay private mortgage insurance.

How Much of Your Income Will the Payment Require?

Typically, lenders will approve home loans that require monthly payments for the combination of the mortgage principal, interest, property taxes, and insurance ("PITI") that total no more than 28 percent of a borrower's monthly gross income, or when combined with other debt payments such as credit card balances, vehicle loans, and student loans, 36 percent of monthly gross income. In some cases, lenders will raise those ratios.

However, our recommendation is to hold off on buying a home if you carry a balance on your credit cards. Tacking a home loan onto these other debts makes it very difficult to give generously, save adequately, and live with your financial margin. Our further recommendation is to take out a mortgage requiring no more than 25 percent of your monthly gross income for the combination of mortgage principal, interest, taxes, and insurance.

Can You Afford the Total Cost of Home Ownership?

For renters, an appliance that stops working or a leaky pipe means calling the landlord to make (and pay for) the repair. For owners, such problems mean out-of-pocket expenses. There are a lot of costs that come with home ownership—from relatively small expenses such as the annual maintenance of your furnace and air conditioner, to much larger expenses such as the replacement of your home's roof—and lots of other costs in between.

You should factor in at least $100 per month for home maintenance and basic repairs. And, you should consider what might need replacing and begin building savings for such items. If you cannot afford to allocate $100 per month of cash flow to maintenance and basic repairs and to save for bigger-ticket replacement items each month (as much as $100–$200 per month, depending on what may need replacing and when), you cannot afford to buy a home.

How Long Will You Live There?

A generally accepted rule of thumb is that you need to live in a home you purchase for five to seven years in order to recoup the costs of buying. There are a variety of up-front expenses involved in buying, moving in, and "making the home your own." And there are costs associated with selling. So, if there's a good chance you will need or want to move sooner than that, you may be better off renting.

Saving on Utility Expenses

The month-after-month savings on utility costs can be an excellent example of the cumulative effect of little things over an extended period of time.

Here are a few ideas for saving on utility expenses:

- Shop around for the best telephone, wireless, and internet plans.
- Be diligent in minimizing energy and water usage.
- Turn off lights when not in use.
- Replace incandescent bulbs with LED light bulbs.
- Set the thermostat higher in summer and lower in winter.
- Use a programmable thermostat.
- Be sure weather stripping is in good shape.
- Conserve water use.

Financial Advantages of Buying a Smaller Home

Persons A and B are both approved for a $180,000 thirty-year mortgage at 7 percent interest and have $45,000 as a down payment. Person A decides to buy a home for $225,000 (the maximum they are approved for—$180,000 mortgage plus $45,000 down payment). Person B decides to buy a less expensive home for $175,000 but to put the same amount down ($45,000) and to make the same mortgage payment as person A.

Let's track their experience:

	Person A	Person B
COST OF HOME	$225,000	$175,000
DOWN PAYMENT	45,000	45,000
MORTGAGE	180,000	130,000
MONTHLY PAYMENT	$1,198	$1,198*
AMT. OWED END OF YEAR 5	$169,437	$98,531

*Required payment=$865/month

After five years, person B sells his home for $175,000, giving him $76,469 cash ($175,000 minus $98,531 owed on his original mortgage). He buys a $225,000 house using the cash as down payment leaving a mortgage of $148,531. He continues to pay $1,198/month toward that mortgage even though his required payments are only $988.

After eighteen more years (twenty-three years after the purchase of the first house), person B's home is paid off. Person B continues to put $1,198/month into a mutual fund returning 10 percent until year thirty. In year thirty, both have their homes paid off but person B also has $143,668 in a mutual fund. You decide: was the five-year wait to get the more expensive home worth it?

Record Keeping

Keeping Year-to-Date Totals on the Spending Record

Often it can be helpful to know how you are doing in various categories not just for the current month but from the beginning of the Spending Plan year.

Lines 4 and 5 on the Spending Record provide that information. Line 4 carries forward the amount each category was over or under the Spending Record from the month before. If this is done each month, and that figure is added to the over or under figure for the current month, the resulting figure represents the status of that category up to this point in the current budget year. In some cases, it may be of little interest to track certain categories because they never vary from budget, and discipline is exercised in those areas. But consider three categories of variable expenses—groceries, clothes, and going out—that have been tracked in the example on page 157.

This current month groceries were $34 under Spending Plan. A total of $480 was allocated but only $446 was spent. In previous months, a total of $218 (line 4) less than what had been allocated was actually spent. That amount, added to the $34 under for this month, gives a Year-to-Date (YTD) total of $252 under the budget (line 5). The food category is in good shape for the year.

The clothes category is $35 over budget for this month and $142 over for the year at the end of last month. As a result, this category is now $177 over for the year to date.

The going out category is $13 under the allotment for this month but was $96 over the allotment prior to this month. That means this category is $83 over the budget for the year.

This cumulative data can be very helpful as the year progresses. In this situation, if the holiday season were approaching, money would be available in the grocery category to have guests over for some nice holiday meals and still stay within the food budget for the year.

On the other hand, since the clothes category is over budget, it might be a good idea to pass the hint to others that it would be nice to get clothing gifts for Christmas!

Moderation in the "going out" category is also needed in order to bring that Spending Plan category back into budget.

MONTH: *January*

		Daily Variable Expenses							Professional Services	Entertainment		
Transportation		**Household**										
Gas, etc.	Maint./Repair	Groceries	Clothes	Gifts	Household Items	Personal	Other		Going Out	Travel	Other
(1) Spending Plan												
200	40	480	150	80	75	50	---	---	100	70	40
64	21	186	89	17	14	16	25		22	70	22 (sitter)
42		22	46	55	22	18			46		
38		20	50		9				19		
58		172			31						
		18									
		8									
		20									
(2) Total												
202	21	446	185	72	76	34	25	---	87	70	22
(3) (Over)/Under												
(2)	19	34	(35)	8	(1)	16	(25)	---	13	---	18
(4) Last Mo. YTD												
218			(142)						(96)		
(5) This Mo. YTD												
252			(177)						(83)		

1	2	3	4	5	6	7	8	9	10	11	12	13	14	15	16	17	18	19	20	21	22	23	24	25	26	27	28	29	30	31

- Use this page to record expenses that tend to be daily, variable expenses—often the hardest to control.
- Keep receipts throughout the day and record them at the end of each day.
- Total each category at the end of the month (line 2) and compare to the Spending Plan (line 1). Subtracting line 2 from line 1 gives you an (over) or under the budget figure for that month (line 3).
- To verify that you have made each day's entry, cross out the number at the bottom of the page that corresponds to that day's date.
- Optional: If you wish to monitor your progress as you go through the year, you can keep cumulative totals in lines 4 and 5.

Implementation Issues

More than One Paycheck per Month

Item	Spending Plan ($)	1st Paycheck ($)	2nd Paycheck ($)
✓ Giving	350	175	175
✓ Saving	155		155
✓ Mortgage	1100	1100	
✓ Utilities	180		180
✓ Telephone	55		55
✓ Auto Payment	370		370
✓ Debt Repayment	220		220
Clothes	110		110
Gifts	80		80
Gas	150	75	75
Food	460	230	230
Household Misc.	75	50	25
Entertainment	150	75	75
Misc. Small Exp.	45	45	
Total	**3500**	**1750**	**1750**

✓ = Paid by check or electronic withdrawal

Making a one-time plan for how each paycheck will be allocated and simply referring to it each payday can be a wonderful way to ease the anxiety over questions like:

"Which bill do I pay now?" and "Do I have enough for food and gas?"

In the above example, the person receives net take-home pay of $3,500 per month and is paid twice a month ($1,750 per pay period). The first column represents the Spending Plan for this family. They give $350 per month, save $155, have a mortgage payment of $1,100, and so on.

Out of the first paycheck, checks are written or electronic withdrawals are made for half of the monthly giving and for the mortgage. The rest of the check is used for half of the allocation for gas, food, entertainment, a portion of household/miscellaneous, and all of the miscellaneous small cash expenditure allocation.

Out of the second paycheck, checks are written or automatic withdrawals are made for the other half of giving, all short-term savings, utilities, telephone, auto payment, and debt repayment. The remainder of that check covers the rest of gas, food, household items, and entertainment.

In developing such a plan, it may be necessary to adjust some payment dates to balance out payments from the two checks. Once the plan has been devised, a copy can be kept with your checkbook or on your computer, and it will eliminate any question about how each paycheck is to be used.

Money Building Up in Certain Categories

Once you begin placing money for certain categories that tend to build up over time into a short-term savings account, the question arises, "I have this savings account, and it has an amount of money in it, but how do I tell how much is for what category?"

The ledger sheet on page 162 shows an example to help answer this question. It is a ledger for a money market fund that contains short-term savings that have accumulated for several budgeting categories.

At the top, there is a description of the four funds into which money is being deposited each payday. In this case, the money is for emergencies, vacations, gifts, and auto repair. Lines 1 through 6 on the form are explained below.

Line 1 is the balance brought forward ($3,500) from the previous year. Based on the activity of that year, $2,100 of that $3,500 belongs to the Emergency account, $500 belongs to the Vacation account, $300 belongs to the Gift account, and $600 belongs to the Auto Repair account.

Lines 2 through 6 show the activity in the fund for the most recent month. On January 8, Dan bought Wendy a birthday gift. He entered $40 in the Total Balance column with parentheses around it, indicating that it is an amount they need to subtract from the balance because they just spent $40. The $40 was also shown as being spent from the Gift fund

On January 15, Dan got paid. He deposited $235 to the fund, so $235 is shown under the Total Balance column. Of that $235, $100 was for the Emergency fund, $70 was for the Vacation fund, $30 was for the Gift fund, and $35 was for the Auto Repair fund. They show those four figures under each of those funds. Since this was money being added to the funds, the figures do not have parentheses around them.

On January 17, Joe's Transmission Shop hit them hard with a $500 transmission job. They paid that out of their Auto Repair fund.

On January 25, they bought Sam and Mary a wedding present and recorded a $50 deduction from the total column, and a $50 deduction from the gift column.

On January 30, another paycheck was again distributed among the four categories.

The last line shows end-of-the-month totals based on adding and subtracting the transactions. The fund now has a total of $3,380 distributed as shown.

On page 164 is a blank form on which you can set up your own ledger to track savings.

Forms

Included on the following pages are forms you can use in your planning. These include the Debt Reduction Plan, Form for Tracking Short-Term Savings, Envelope Record-Keeping Worksheet, the Spending Plan, and the Spending Record. Additional copies as well as digital versions of many of the forms can be found at abingdonpress.com/savinggrace.

If you decide to use the written record-keeping system, these forms can be used for the next two months. Feel free to make photocopies of a blank Spending Record to use for subsequent months.

WENDY AND DAN'S MARKET FUND FOR SHORT-TERM SAVINGS

MONTH _____

	Date	Description	Total Fund Balance	Fund #1 Emergency	Fund #2 Vacation	Fund #3 Gift	Fund #4 Auto Repair	Fund #5
1	12/31	Previous year balance forward	3500	2100	500	300	600	
2	1/8	Wendy's birthday gift	(40)			(40)		
3	1/15	Paycheck	235	100	70	30	35	
4	1/17	Joe's Transmission Shop	(500)				(500)	
5	1/25	Sam and Mary's Wedding	(50)			(50)		
6	1/30	Paycheck	235	100	70	30	35	
		End of month total	3380	2300	640	270	170	

FORM #1: DEBT REDUCTION PLAN

Item	Amount Owed	Interest	Minimum Monthly Payment $___	Additional Payment	Payment Plan and Pay-off Dates					
Total										

- The first and second columns list to whom the debt is owed and the amount owed. Debts are listed in the order of lowest to highest amount.
- The third and fourth columns list the interest rate and the minimum monthly payment for each debt.
- The fifth column indicates the amount of additional payment above the minimum that can be made and adds that amount to the minimum payment for the first (smallest) debt listed.
- The remaining columns show how, as each debt is paid, the payment for it is rolled down to the next debt. Pay-off dates can be calculated in advance or simply recorded as they are achieved.

Appendix: Implementation Issues ■ 163

FORM #2: FORM FOR TRACKING SHORT-TERM SAVINGS

Month: _____

Date	Description	Total Fund Balance	Fund #1	Fund #2	Fund #3	Fund #4	Fund #5

FORM #3: ENVELOPE RECORD-KEEPING WORKSHEET

Envelope Record-Keeping Worksheet

Envelopes

The boxes below represent envelopes in which you will place cash for variable expenses each month. For each category, write in the category name (clothing, food, etc.) and the budgeted amount.

Category: _____
$ _____

Category: _____
$ _____

Category: _____
$ _____

Category: _____
$ _____

Category: _____
$ _____

Category: _____
$ _____

Category: _____
$ _____

Category: _____
$ _____

Checks/Automatic Withdrawals

Use the entries below to list the regular monthly expenses that you will pay by check or automatic withdrawal.

Category: _____
$ _____

Category: _____
$ _____

Category: _____
$ _____

Category: _____
$ _____

Category: _____
$ _____

Category: _____
$ _____

Category: _____
$ _____

Category: _____
$ _____

FORM #4: SPENDING PLAN

What I Spend

Earnings/Income Per Month	Totals
Salary #1 (net take-home)	_____
Salary #2 (net take-home)	_____
Other (less taxes)	_____
Total Monthly Income	$ _____

% Guide*

1. Giving $ _____

Church _____
Other Contributions _____

2. Savings   15% $ _____

Emergency _____
Replacement _____
Long Term _____

3. Debt   0-10% $ _____

Credit Cards:
   Visa _____
   MasterCard _____
   Discover _____
   American Express _____
   Gas Cards _____
   Department Stores _____
Education Loans _____
Other Loans:
   Bank Loans _____
   Credit Union _____
   Family/Friends _____
   Other _____

4. Housing   25-36% $ _____

Mortgage/Taxes/Rent _____
Maintenance/Repairs _____
Utilities:
   Electric _____
   Gas _____
   Water _____
   Trash and Recycling _____
   Telephone/Internet _____
   TV/Streaming Services _____
   Other _____

5. Auto/Transp.   15-20% $ _____

Car Payments/License _____
Gas & Bus/Train/Parking _____
Oil/Lube/Maintenance _____

*This is a percent of total monthly income. These are guidelines only and may be different for individual situations. However, there should be good rationale for a significant variance.

6. Insurance (Paid by you)   5% $ _____

Auto _____
Homeowners _____
Life _____
Medical/Dental _____
Other _____

7. Household/Personal   15-25% $ _____

Groceries _____
Clothes/Dry Cleaning _____
Gifts _____
Household Items _____
Personal:
   Tobacco & Alcohol _____
   Cosmetics _____
   Barber/Beauty _____
Other:
   Books/Magazines/Music _____
   Allowances _____
   Personal Technology _____
   Extracurricular Activities _____
   Education _____
   Pets _____
   Miscellaneous _____

8. Entertainment   5-10% $ _____

Going Out:
   Meals _____
   Movies/Events _____
   Babysitting _____
Travel (Vacation/Trips) _____
Other:
   Fitness/Sports _____
   Hobbies _____
   Media Subscriptions _____
   Other _____

9. Prof. Services   5-15% $ _____

Child Care _____
Medical/Dental/Prescriptions _____
Other:
   Legal _____
   Counseling _____
   Professional Dues _____

10. Misc. Small Cash Expenditures   2-3% $ _____

Total Expenses $ _____

TOTAL MONTHLY INCOME	$ _____
LESS TOTAL EXPENSES	$ _____
INCOME OVER/(UNDER) EXPENSES	$ _____

FORM #5: SPENDING RECORD

MONTH: _____

Daily Variable Expenses

	Transportation		Household						Professional Services	Entertainment		
	Gas, etc.	Maint./ Repair	Groceries	Clothes	Gifts	Household Items	Personal	Other		Going Out	Travel	Other
(1) Spending Plan												
1												
2												
3												
4												
5												
6												
7												
8												
9												
10												
11												
12												
13												
14												
15												
16												
17												
18												
19												
20												
21												
22												
23												
24												
25												
26												
27												
28												
29												
30												
31												
(2) Total												
(3) (Over)/Under												
(4) Last Mo. YTD												
(5) This Mo. YTD												

- Use this page to record expenses that tend to be daily, variable expenses—often the hardest to control.
- Keep receipts throughout the day and record them at the end of each day.
- Total each category at the end of the month (line 2) and compare to the Spending Plan (line 1). Subtracting line 2 from line 1 gives you an (over) or under the budget figure for that month (line 3).
- To verify that you have made each day's entry, cross out the number at the bottom of the page that corresponds to that day's date.
- Optional: If you wish to monitor your progress as you go through the year, you can keep cumulative totals in lines 4 and 5.

FORM #5: SPENDING RECORD

MONTH: _____

Monthly Regular Expenses (generally paid by check once a month)

	Giving		Savings	Debt			Housing				Auto Payments	Insurance		Misc. Cash Expenses
	Church	Other		Credit Cards	Education	Other	Mortgage/ Rent	Maintenance	Utilities	Other		Auto/ Home	Life/ Medical	
(1) Spending Plan														
(2) Total														
(3) (Over)/Under														
(4) Last Mo. YTD														
(5) This Mo. YTD														

- This page allows you to record major monthly expenses for which you typically write just one or two checks per month.
- Entries can be recorded as the checks are written (preferably) or by referring back to the check ledger at a convenient time.
- Total each category at the end of the month (line 2) and compare to the Spending Plan (line 1). Subtracting line 2 from line 1 gives you an (over) or under the budget figure for that month (line 3).
- Use the "Monthly Assessment" section to reflect on the future actions that will be helpful in staying on course.

MONTHLY ASSESSMENT

Area	(Over)/Under	Reason	Future Action

Areas of Victory _____

Areas to Watch _____

Benefits and Services for United Methodist Clergy

United Methodist clergy often have access to certain employee benefits and financial planning resources through the denomination or their annual conferences. Following is a brief overview of some of these benefits and services. For more detailed information, contact Wespath at https://www.wespath.org, or 1-800-851-2201 or your conference benefits officer.

- Clergy in the United States appointed full-time as United Methodist local church pastors, district superintendents, and conference or district staff typically have retirement benefits through a U.S.-wide clergy retirement plan, currently the Clergy Retirement Security Program (CRSP). CRSP combines a defined benefit providing lifetime income based on years of service to the church with a defined contribution account that you can access in retirement as your needs require. Your church or conference contributes an amount equal to 2 percent of your compensation to this account. Some annual conferences provide CRSP for clergy appointed ¾-time or ½-time.

- The United Methodist Personal Investment Plan (UMPIP) is a 403(b) retirement savings plan for United Methodist churches, general agencies, and other church-related organizations. Clergy can make before-tax or Roth contributions through payroll deductions and may receive plan retirement contributions from their local church, conference, or employer. Clergy who contribute at least 1 percent of compensation to UMPIP receive an additional 1 percent matching contribution in their CRSP defined contribution accounts.

- The Comprehensive Protection Plan (CPP) provides death benefits, long-term disability income, and certain other survivor benefits for clergy appointed full-time to local churches, annual conferences, districts, and general agencies. Some annual conferences extend CPP coverage to clergy appointed ¾-time. Clergy appointed to other United Methodist employers may also have CPP benefits if those employers elect to sponsor the plan. The CPP death benefit for active clergy is $50,000, and therefore, as noted in the "Other Benefits" section, is a tax-free benefit.

- Clergy with UMPIP or CRSP defined contribution retirement account balances at Wespath can elect to have the investment of those accounts managed automatically at no additional cost by Wespath's LifeStage Investment Management service. LifeStage Investment Management allocates your account balances among selected investment funds to create a target investment mix based on your age, risk tolerance, whether you qualify for Social Security benefits, and other factors. Each quarter, LifeStage Investment Management compares your target mix with your actual mix of investments, which changes due to market fluctuations. If there is a significant difference, the service will automatically rebalance your current investment mix and future allocations.

- Financial planning services are available to United Methodist active clergy and other participants in Wespath-administered plans through an arrangement with EY Financial Planning Services. There is no direct charge to the clergyperson for EY's services, as the costs are included in Wespath's operating expenses. EY financial planning assistance is confidential and objective, as the EY financial planners do not sell investment or insurance products. Clergy can call EY directly at 1-800-360-2539. Additional financial planning tools and resources are available through the EY Navigate website, https://wespath.eynavigate.com.

As stated previously, the terrain for clergy finances shifts frequently, and it is therefore important to monitor tax laws and changes in denominational pension and benefit plans. This is certainly true for The United Methodist Church, where both the annual conference and the denomination may make changes in benefits from time to time. For example, a proposal going to the next General Conference calls for replacing CRSP as of January 1, 2023, with an account balance-based retirement plan. When in doubt about benefits and related services, contact your conference benefits officer or Wespath for current information.

Notes

Chapter 3

1. John Wesley, Sermon 50, "The Use of Money," II, 1, http://wesley.nnu.edu/john-wesley/the-sermons-of-john-wesley-1872-edition/sermon-50-the-use-of-money/. Accessed July 26, 2020.
2. John Wesley, Sermon 50, "The Use of Money," II, 5. Accessed July 26, 2020.
3. John Wesley, Sermon 50, "The Use of Money," III, 4. Accessed July 26, 2020.

Chapter 4

1. John Wesley, Sermon 29, "Sermon on the Mount: Discourse Nine," 17, http://wesley.nnu.edu/john-wesley/the-sermons-of-john-wesley-1872-edition/sermon-29-upon-our-lords-sermon-on-the-mount-discourse-nine/. Accessed July 26, 2020.
2. John Wesley, Sermon 126, "On the Danger of Increasing Riches," 11, 2, http://wesley.nnu.edu/john-wesley/the-sermons-of-john-wesley-1872-edition/sermon-126-on-the-danger-of-increasing-riches/. Accessed July 26, 2020.
3. "Average U.S. Credit Card Debt in 2020," https://www.magnifymoney.com/blog/news/u-s-credit-card-debt-by-the-numbers628618371/. Accessed July 27, 2020.

Chapter 5

1. John Wesley, Sermon 50, "The Use of Money," III, 4. Accessed July 26, 2020.
2. Josh Moody, "Where the Top Fortune 500 CEOs Attended College," *US News & World Reports*, published June 10, 2020, https://www.usnews.com/education/best-colleges/articles/where-the-top-fortune-500-ceos-attended-college. Accessed July 29, 2020.